Great Historical Enterprises

*

Problems in Monastic
History

Great Historical Enterprises

*

Problems in Monastic History

David Knowles

Thomas Nelson and Sons Ltd
London Edinburgh Paris Melbourne Johannesburg
Toronto and New York

THOMAS NELSON AND SONS LTD
Parkside Works Edinburgh 9
36 Park Street London W1
117 Latrobe Street Melbourne C1

THOMAS NELSON AND SONS (AFRICA) (Pty) LTD
P.O. Box 9881 Johannesburg

THOMAS NELSON AND SONS (CANADA) LTD
91–93 Wellington Street West   Toronto 1

THOMAS NELSON AND SONS
18 East 41st Street New York 17, N.Y.

SOCIÉTÉ FRANÇAISE D'ÉDITIONS NELSON
97 rue Monge Paris 5

Preface

THE first part of this book consists of a sequence of addresses, with the general title 'Great Historical Enterprises,' delivered before the Royal Historical Society. Requests for their publication in book form have been made repeatedly, and I wish to thank Council of that Society for allowing me to reprint them.

For his kindness in reading in typescript the paper on The Bollandists and for suggesting many emendations I am indebted to Père Paul Grosjean, S.J. Professor Walther Holtzmann, Director of the German Historical Institute at Rome, and a member of the Zentraldirektion of the *Monumenta*, was kind enough to read the draft of the lecture on the *Monumenta Germaniae Historica* and to make a number of corrections and suggestions. While warmly thanking Dr Holtzmann, I must also make it clear that the opinions and judgments (and possible errors) are mine, not his. For my lecture on the Rolls Series I should like to thank the late Keeper of the Records, Sir David Evans, for his kindness and gratefully to acknowledge the help of Mr H. C. Johnson, Miss D. H. Gifford and others in facilitating my research at the Public Record Office.

The second part contains the substance of the Birkbeck Lectures as delivered at Cambridge in the Lent Term of 1962, and I may be allowed once more to express my thanks to the Master and Council

of Trinity College for inviting me to join the company
of ecclesiastical historians who have in the past given
lustre to this foundation.

The topics discussed may seem from their titles
to be arid and remote, but there is much of historical
and even, to my mind, of human interest—of the
dignity as well as of the comedy of human beings—
in the story of these four great enterprises, from
which historians and students have derived, and continue to derive, so much benefit. As for the critical
problems connected with the early documents of the
traditional Benedictine and the reformed Cistercian
ways of monastic life, they have, besides their real
importance in religious history, much of the perennial
appeal of the historical mystery, not to say, of the
detective story.

In addition, these two groups of studies show in
their different ways what critical methods of historical
research can achieve: the one by presenting the
records of the past to modern students as accurately
and completely as possible, the other by wresting
from those records a portion of historical truth that
had been hidden for many centuries.

In conclusion, it is a pleasure to thank my friend
Dr H. P. Morrison for his kindness in inviting me to
publish these pages under the imprint of that distinguished house whose reputation in the world of
letters and learning has never been higher than under
his enlightened direction.

DAVID KNOWLES

Peterhouse, Cambridge
July 1962

Contents

Abbreviations

Acta SS.	*Acta Sanctorum* (Bollandist)
A.D.B.	*Allgemeine Deutsche Biographie*
B.N.	Bibliothèque Nationale
B.M.	British Museum
CC	*Carta Caritatis*
C.O.C.R.	*Collectanea ordinis Cisterciensium Reformatorum*
D.A.	*Deutsches Archiv*
D.A.C.	*Dictionnaire d'archéologie chrétienne et de liturgie*
D.K.	Deputy Keeper of the Public Records
D.N.B.	*Dictionary of National Biography*
EC	*Exordium Cistercii*
EM	*Exordium Magnum*
EP	*Exordium Parvum*
H.M.S.O.	His (Her) Majesty's Stationery Office
LB	Letter Book (at P.R.O.)
M.G.H.	*Monumenta Germaniae Historica*
MP	*Monuments primitifs de la règle cistercienne*, ed. Guignard
M.R.	Master of the Rolls
N.A.	*Neues Archiv*
N.D.B.	*Neue Deutsche Biographie*
P.L.	*Patrologia Latina*
P.R.O.	Public Record Office
Q (QQ)	Question(s) in public inquiry
R.A.M.	*Revue d'ascétique et de mystique*
R.B.	*Rule of St Benedict*
Rev.Bén.	*Revue Bénédictine*
R.H.E.	*Revue d'histoire ecclésiastique*
RM	*Regula Magistri*
RS	Rolls Series
R.T.A.M.	*Recherches de théologie ancienne et médiévale*
S.M.	*Studien und Mitteilungen zur Geschichte des Benediktinerordens*
St.Ans.	*Studia Anselmiana*
T.C.D.	Trinity College Dublin

Great
Historical Enterprises

*

The Bollandists

There is no full-scale history of the Bollandists. There are several authoritative articles in encyclopedias etc., of which the best are perhaps those by Ch. De Smedt in the *Catholic Encyclopedia* (1907) and A. de Bil in the *Dictionnaire d'histoire et de géographie ecclésiastiques* (1937). To these may be added the section on the Bollandists in R. Aigrain, *L'Hagiographie* (Paris 1953), pp. 329–50, which is largely a précis of Delehaye's account (below). The reader who wishes for an approach which is at once broader and more intimate will find it in three historical essays by modern Bollandists: *A travers trois siècles: L'Œuvre des Bollandistes*, 1615–1915, by H. Delehaye (Brussels 1920); *L'Œuvre des Bollandistes* (Mémoires de l'Académie Royale de Belgique, Classe des Lettres, tome xxxix, fascicule 4, 1942), by P. Peeters, and the same writer's 'Après un siècle (1837–1937),' in *Analecta Bollandiana*, LV, pp. iv–xliv. To these should be added, for Bollandists of the past, the memoirs published from time to time in the *Acta Sanctorum*, and articles in *Biographie Nationale* by A. Poncelet, H. Delehaye and others; and for more recent personalities the biographical sketches by P. Peeters, reprinted from the *Analecta*, in *Figures Bollandiennes contemporaines* (sc. Ch. De Smedt, A. Poncelet, J. Van den Gheyn, F. Van Ortroy and H. Delehaye), published in Brussels, 1948, and the same writer's 'Notice sur la vie et les travaux du R. P. H. Delehaye,' in *Annuaire de l'Académie Royale de Belgique* (1943). Finally, there is the memoir of P. Peeters himself by P. Devos in *Analecta Bollandiana*, LXIX (1951), pp. i–xlvii. All the above sources, it will be noted, are works by the Bollandists themselves, or are based upon these, as is likewise the present paper. Indeed, no scholar from outside the house could have access to the essential records and papers. It will, however, be appreciated that a domestic history, however scholarly and candid, cannot be expected to see Bollandism as it appears *ab extra* and in the round.

I

The Bollandists

ON several occasions during the last twenty or
thirty years students of the past have had their
attention directed to the seventeenth century by
historians of science and of scholarship. We have
been told that we shall find there the authentic
beginnings of the modern world, and that in that age
reliance on the traditions and books of the past gives
way to experiment, to analysis and to criticism. In
the realm of history, there is a shift from the classical,
literary traditions to the original sources and to
official records, while the historical writings of the
past are subjected to the new technique which for a
hundred years had been applied to the literary
masterpieces of the ancient world by a succession of
great scholars from Valla and Erasmus to Scaliger
and Casaubon. Certainly, in many ways the seventeenth century is more significant in the annals of
historiography than is the century that followed. In
England, it is the age of Dodsworth, Dugdale,
Twysden, Wharton, Wanley and Hearne. In France,
it is the age of D'Achery, Labbé, Ducange and the
Maurists. In the part of the Netherlands that is now
Belgium, it is the age of the first Bollandists.

For the moment it is with these last alone that we
are concerned. They take pride of place for two good
reasons. Theirs was the first great enterprise of

co-operative scholarship in the modern world; and
theirs is the only enterprise of the seventeenth century
which still continues in active function. What is more
remarkable, in all essentials both of spirit and of out-
ward form it still remains a recognizable descendant
of its first parents. It still remains, what it always has
been, a small unofficial group of Jesuits of the territories roughly coincident with modern Belgium,[1]
living together in a single establishment for years or
for life, devoted solely to the collection and publication of the original sources for the lives of the saints.
How did this group arise, and how continue?

The begetter of the idea, though not of the institute, was Héribert Roswey or, as he is usually called,
Rosweyde, a native of Utrecht (1569–1629).[2] As a
young Jesuit professor of philosophy Rosweyde had
occupied his leisure in examining and copying
manuscripts in the ancient abbeys of Flanders.
Among these were many lives of the saints, ancient
and medieval. Rosweyde was familiar with the
collections of saints' lives current from medieval
times and augmented and republished since the

---

[1] An absolutely accurate statement would be more complicated. From
1612 to 1773 there were two Belgian provinces, *Flandro-Belgica* and *Gallo-
Belgica*, covering an area greater than modern Belgium, and the Bollandists
were recruited from the former of these. From 1832 to 1929 modern
Belgium (with Luxembourg) formed a single province, which in 1929
was divided into two, northern and southern, both of which now supply
recruits.

[2] For Rosweyde, see Ch. De Smedt, 'Les fondateurs du Bollandisme,'
in *Mélanges Godefroid Kurth*, I, pp. 295–9, and A. Poncelet in *Biographie
Nationale*, xx, cols. 170–8. For the religious background, see A. Poncelet,
Histoire de la Compagnie de Jésus dans les Pays-Bas (Brussels 1928).
Rosweyde also published a series of Lives of the Saints for each day of
the year, translated into Flemish.

Renaissance; in these, and in the separate lives of
individuals, the historical figure, the human personality, was lost beneath layers of legend and rhetoric,
or diluted to insipidity by imagination and error.
Rosweyde conceived the idea of collecting all the
authentic documents, to be criticized and explained
with the technique of scholarship recently applied
so successfully to Sophocles and Sallust. He was
a practical man; he roughed out a prospectus for
eighteen volumes in 1607 and sent it to a number of
scholars and ecclesiastical authorities. Among those
whom he approached was the great luminary of his
own order, the illustrious theologian and contro-
versialist, now himself among the saints, Cardinal
Robert Bellarmine. Bellarmine, though personally
familiar with laborious days, had no illusions, and
came out flat against the scheme; not only was it
impracticable, but those old lives of the saints,
incredible and often ridiculous as they were, would
be much better left unpublished. Others, however,
were less discouraging. Rosweyde's own provincial,
and an official representative of the general Aquaviva,
gave him their blessing, and he found a faithful
patron in the Benedictine abbot of Liessies, third
successor of the saintly Blosius, Louis de Blois. In
later years the Bollandists showed their gratitude by
including a life of the uncanonized Blosius in the
January *Acta*; they had also the satisfaction of heaping coals of fire on another head when Bellarmine
joined the ranks of the *beati*. Meanwhile Rosweyde,
not content with a prospectus, provided posterity
with two strangely apt samples of the kind of thing

he wished to see done: the first (1613) an edition of
the Roman Martyrology, followed by one of the *Vetus
Romanum*; the second (1615) an edition of the *Vitae
Patrum*, the lives and sayings of the Fathers of the
Desert. In the first he drove hard under full sail at a
reef-strown passage which his followers were to be
three centuries in charting; in the other he gave them
not only a priceless indication of method but also a
legacy of the purest spiritual tradition, which his
contemporaries took to themselves in a book which
was a classic from the first and has proved its worth
even in our own days.[1] Then, after a shower of other
publications, Rosweyde gave his final lesson to posterity by dying a *martyr caritatis* in 1629 of a disease
contracted at the bedside of a dying penitent.

Rosweyde left behind him the memory of a good
life, a large collection of transcripts, a great book
and a germinal idea. Before accepting a total aban-
donment of his familiar project, the superiors of his
order decided to send an energetic young man to sift
his literary remains. The young man's name was John
Bolland (1596–1665)[2]; he was a native of the modern
province of Liège, and the family house in which he
was born was to be seen till 1914, when it disappeared
when the village was burnt by the German army.
Bolland reported that if the papers were collected
and worked over, Rosweyde's scheme could be
executed without undue delay, though not without

---

[1] As, for example, in the extracts so felicitously translated by Miss
Helen Waddell in *The Desert Fathers* (1936).
[2] A memoir, *De vita, operibus et virtutibus Joannis Bollandi*, by
D. Papebroch, is in *Acta SS.*, t. 1 Martii.

considerable labour. He also gave it to be understood that if the toil were imposed upon him he
would not seek to avoid it. The provincial of Flandro-
Belgica accepted both the report and the offer;
Bolland was appointed confessor and spiritual
director of the house of professed Jesuits at Antwerp
with the commission to execute Rosweyde's plan in
his hours of leisure. He himself, always methodical,
there and then laid his plans for his own further
studies in other equally important subjects when he
should have accomplished his task. 'Fortunately,'
Papebroch was to remark, 'neither Bolland nor
Father Provincial had the faintest idea of what they
had undertaken to do.' As a modern Bollandist has
put it, they crossed the Rubicon without noticing
that it was there.

Once at work, Bolland found both that Rosweyde's plan must be extended, and that the material
both old and new was more copious than he had
realized. Without help or funds he would die on the
task. Funds were supplied by the same abbot who
had helped Rosweyde; a helper was to hand in an
old pupil of Bolland, Godefroid Henskens or, as he
was called, Henschenius (1601–81).[1] It was an ideal
combination. Both were men of brazen sinews capable of prodigies of industry and endurance; both
were excellent scholars of the type produced all over
Europe by the new model of the great Jesuit edu-
cators; Bolland had no fear of responsibilities and
decisions, while Henskens was loyalty and modesty

[1] Papebroch contributed a memoir of Henskens in *Acta SS.*, t. VII
Maii.

personified. If Bolland was the founder of the *Acta Sanctorum* Henskens was the first Bollandist. It was he who transformed a partnership into a society, an undertaking into a living tradition; he handed on to the next generation an *esprit de corps*, or rather what we should call a family spirit.

Eight years after the arrival of Henskens the first volumes appeared, 2,500 folio pages, containing the lives of saints whose memory received liturgical commemoration in the month of January. Before continuing the history of the project we may pause a moment to consider its nature and design.

This is not the place to discuss the value, or the interest to the world, of hagiography in general. It is more appropriate to remark that it would be hard to think of any field of critical or historical research that could prove more fruitful in every kind of problem, or one in which a greater variety of skills and disciplines could be employed. The well-documented lives of the eminent saints of modern and medieval times are possibly no more difficult to present in authentic form than are those of other celebrities, though a brief study of the complex critical questions surrounding the early lives of St Francis of Assisi in the thirteenth century or the autobiography of St Thérèse of Lisieux in our own day might make us chary of being too certain about this. 'Straight' lives, however, are only a fragment of the mass. What is a saint? Who were saints? What are the tests for sifting out bogus, ghost and bilocating saints? What acid tests are to be applied to Charlemagne, a place-name or a consul who have all
(2,619)

arrived at some kind of liturgical commemoration? The hagiographer is plunged at once into the nightmare of early medieval diplomatic and forgery, into all the tangled chronological difficulties of the *fasti* of half the sees of Europe, into the labyrinthine ways of martyrologies, necrologies and calendars, into the linguistic, social and psychological varieties of Christian sentiment—Greek, Persian, Egyptian, Syrian, Slav and Oriental, into the magical mists and colours of the Celtic wonderland, and into the changes and translations that lapse of centuries and popular devotion can bring about in a matter that is of its nature peculiarly dependent upon personal knowledge and popular acclaim. If we add to all this the theological background and the judgment of credibility, possibility and moral and spiritual sanity inseparable from the subject-matter—the *ex-hypothesi* acceptance that the historian is often dealing with a personality which is in some or many ways abnormal or supranormal or both—we shall begin to realize that the sober and laborious Jean Bolland need not have feared that he would lack for mental occupation in his old age.

To the intrinsic difficulties of the subject-matter were added the difficulties inseparable from the plan adopted. Rosweyde had assumed, and Bolland had accepted, a treatment according to the order of the calendar: that is, the hagiographers were to work through the liturgical year dealing with the saints commemorated on each day, whether now or in the past, by at least one of the churches or institutes of Christendom. Once granted that the work was to be

more than a summary of existing knowledge the difficulties of this arrangement become only too obvious.
Every week, almost every day, saints are commemorated from almost every age and region; the hagiographer must be a polymath. On the other hand,
saints closely associated in life (St Francis and
St Clare, another St Francis and St Jane Frances
de Chantal), saints of the same order (St Stephen
Harding and St Bernard), saints of the same city
(St Augustine of Canterbury and his immediate successors), are often separated by half the calendar
year. The hagiographer must again and again leave
unexploited a field which he has mastered, and which
another a generation later must bring again laboriously
under cultivation.[1] Yet it is difficult to see what other
arrangement could have been made. Any chronological or alphabetic arrangement, besides being
equally artificial, would from the start have post-
poned indefinitely any kind of publication with a
general appeal; it would moreover have entailed,
even in the seventeenth century, an incalculable
amount of preparatory work with nothing to show
for it. All existing lists of saints ancient and modern
were tied to the calendar, and liturgical commemoration was the ultimate touchstone of acceptance
for all saints living before the standardization in the
twelfth century of the canonical process of canonization. The calendar therefore was, and is, the Bollandist framework, but it had its limitations and
drawbacks. Bolland can be forgiven for failing to

---

[1] In the most recent volumes, more than a hundred names appear
each day among those *praetermissi et in alios dies relati*.

realize that his text of the life of Ailred would prove
susceptible of considerable improvement three centuries later, or that those who first read that improved
text would have all passed away long before the name
of St Thomas of Canterbury was reached, but even
Bolland must sometimes have conceived what must
be the unspoken wish of every good Bollandist—that
the reigning pontiff would put a moratorium of
indefinite length upon all processes of canonization.

In any case the distant future was hidden from
Bolland and Henskens, and after fifteen further years
of labour the saints of February appeared in three
volumes in 1658. They were received with universal
applause, and Bolland was rewarded by an invitation
to Rome from Pope Alexander VII. The journey was
too much for his physical powers; it had however
been clear for some time that before more volumes
were published an extensive combing of the libraries
of Europe was a necessity, and Bolland decided to
dispatch his colleague on a quest for manuscripts
that should include Rome as a port of call; as a companion he sent with him the promising son of parents
who had long been among his penitents at Antwerp,
and in whom the ageing scholar had long seen the
child of his desire. In 1659 the mature young Daniel
Van Papenbroeck (1628–1714) had been assigned to
the *Acta Sanctorum*.[1]

If Henschenius was the first Bollandist, Papebroch was to be for all time the type and finest
flower of the genus. To a native capacity for fine

[1] For Papebroch, see the memoir in *Acta SS.*, t. VI Junii, and
H. Delehaye in *Biographie Nationale*, XVI.

scholarship and remorseless industry, to a frank, humble and kindly nature, he had added a solid piety and a conviction of conscience that his work was worthy of his uttermost effort, and should absorb all his energies. He was in addition a man of wide views, with his fair share of the good fortune that so often seems to accompany genius; the document he wanted seemed to lie under the first stone he turned. Finally—and this is perhaps the specific difference of a Bollandist among scholars—he saw historic truth as a Dominican sees theological truth, as a reflection of Truth itself perceptible by the intellect, and as something to be freed from and defended against every attempt to cloud or to confuse it. He never confused the accidental with the essential, and he had a clear and persuasive gift of exposition.

Henskens and Papebroch left Antwerp at the end of July 1660 on what was the first of the *voyages littéraires* which twenty years later were to have their culmination in the celebrated pilgrimages of Mabillon in 1685 and Martène a little later. Papebroch, like others engaged upon the Grand Tour, kept a careful diary. They were absent for two years and five months, during which they perambulated south Germany, the Austrian Tyrol, Italy from Trent to Naples, and the length of France. Twelve months or more were spent in two long sojourns in Rome, where Alexander VII did all he could to open stiff doors and persuade or compel surly librarians and jealous *dilettanti* to uncover their treasures. The two Jesuits were not without funds and were able everywhere to set copyists at work; they returned with 1,400 lives of saints and for several years their scribes continued to add to the number. The voyage, besides providing countless new friends and subscribers, had an important consequence for the *Acta*; the travellers realized that Greek lives must be included in their programme, and when the March volumes appeared there were for the first time columns of Greek type. Journeys of this kind were repeated during the next fifty years, but even more valuable was the help given by friends and confrères in the Jesuit houses up and down Europe, which acted as factories to supply the raw material for the workshop at Antwerp.

Not long after the return of the travellers the venerable founder of the work died at the age of sixty-nine (1665). His death was followed after a short interval by that of Henskens with a tale (more seemly for a Bollandist) of eighty-one years (1681). He had assisted in the production of twenty-four volumes, some of them posthumous; it was a record which even Papebroch failed to break and one which, it may be confidently asserted, will remain unbroken to the end of time, whether or not the *Acta* are still in progress at that moment. After the death of Bolland the little group had adopted the unwritten constitution that still governs the work: labour completely in common regulated by free discussion; decisions taken together according to the traditional customs of the house; no leader or superior, but the senior in years for the time being acting as *primus inter pares*. The actual workshop, which had for

Bolland lain in an attic of the college, came to be the library, the Museum Bollandianum with its fabled cupboard of three hundred and sixty-five drawers,[1] though later each of the collaborators had a study of his own.

With the death of Henschenius there began the long and irregular succession of new arrivals in the Museum. Some proved unfit or unwilling; some died young, carried off by consumption or, like Rosweyde, victims to their priestly charity in times of plague. One or two in each generation rose above the others to give a character to the work. The fifty-four years in which Papebroch was active were in some ways the richest period of all the pre-Revolutionary era, and competent judges have pronounced the eighteen-odd volumes to which he contributed to be the most important of the series; they were those of March, April, May and early June. In the course of his researches he had encountered wraiths and monsters as varied and hideous as ever confronted Beowulf. Some were in full vigour, others already mortally wounded by earlier knights-errant, and others again mere twittering shades. The Acts of St Silvester, the missionary journey of Lazarus and the three Marys, Denys the Areopagite in his various avatars and with his portable head; the dragons of St George and St Theodore, St Luke's portraits of Our Lady— these are only a few samples of the apparitions that whiffled through the thickets of hagiology. Papebroch was no sceptic, no Hardouin; nor did he, as

---

[1] February has only twenty-eight days in the Roman calendar followed by the Bollandists.

did that lamented Bollandist *in partibus*, Herbert Thurston, seem to take an impish delight in shocking the devotee, but he had no mercy for what he proved false by legitimate criticism, and he did not hold that a historical or critical argument could never be more than a probable one, or that a false or superstitious tradition, however venerable or harmless, should be allowed to pass as authentic. In the sequel, Papebroch did not escape attacks, and in the storm that followed, the *Acta Sanctorum* came near foundering. The turn of the seventeenth century was a time of peculiarly acrid controversy in ecclesiastical circles. Jansenism, Probabilism, Quietism and Gallicanism were embittering the waters, and the papacy was in a delicate position with regard both to France and to Spain. Bayle and Fontenelle were inaugurating the age of reason and enlightenment. The Jesuits had many enemies, who would not rest till they had the Society on the ground.

The specific *casus belli* was the treatment by the Bollandists of the origins of the Carmelite order.[1] According to their own story, the white friars derived ultimately from the disciples of the prophet Elijah, whose successors on Carmel at the dawn of the Christian era had been the first clients of the Blessed Virgin. Papebroch, in his treatment of St Berthold in March and of St Albert of Jerusalem in April, duly recorded the lack of historical evidence for this tradition. The Carmelites took offence, and for some

---

[1] This episode in particular would clearly demand much careful and critical research before the whole story could be put fairly in its contemporary setting.

twenty years continued their attacks upon the Bollandists. Finally, the *Acta* of March, April and May were denounced secretly to the Spanish Inquisition, who proceeded to condemn them as erroneous, heretical, offensive to pious ears and schismatical. Shortly afterwards, a similar condemnation was solicited in Rome by the Belgian provincial of the Carmelites, who drew up a comprehensive catalogue of the hoary legends that had received their *coup de grâce* in the *Acta*, and demanded satisfaction from Pope Innocent XII. This request met with a very modified success. The pope himself was unmoved, but the political situation made a collision with Spain inadvisable, and the enemies of Papebroch succeeded in persuading the responsible official to put the introductory volume of May, which contained some sharp words about papal elections of the past, upon the Roman Index, where it remained until the days of Leo XIII. Meanwhile the Bollandists were active in self-defence both in Spain and Rome. In the former country, where Jesuit influence was strong, they succeeded after twenty years (1715) in obtaining a complete reversal of the censure of the Inquisition. At Rome, where they enjoyed the personal friendship of successive popes, their cause was ably defended by one of their number, Janninck,[1] and they were never in serious danger. Papebroch, who had not unnaturally been deeply moved by the attack upon his work and still more by the slur upon his orthodoxy, appealed personally and solemnly to the pope for redress, but he died before full justice was done to

---

[1] Memoir in *Acta SS.*, t. III Julii.

his name. The enemies who had hoped to strangle the *Acta* were disappointed in their hopes, but they had at least achieved the unfortunate result of slowing down the Bollandists for almost twenty years, while they defended themselves and their methods, and of making the next generation, which had no Papebroch to set the tone, less outspoken and often somewhat ambivalent in their conclusions.

Papebroch died in 1714 in his eighty-seventh year. He has rightly been considered by subsequent generations of Bollandists as the mightiest of their line, carrying up to an eminent degree the industry, the intellectual honesty, the modesty and the piety of his tribe, and adding to it the touch of genius that makes him the peer of his greatest contemporaries such as Mabillon, Ducange, Grotius, Leibniz and Bentley. No successor appeared to wear his mantle. The leader of the group for twenty years after his death was Du Sollier,[1] a scholar of parts and an able administrator; he retired in 1736 and died four years later, having produced an excellent edition of the martyrology of Usuard, and put both the domestic arrangements and the typography of the *Acta* into better trim. He had in full measure the methodical industry of the house; he always took copies with his own hands of his manuscript letters; at his death more than 12,000 of these were found among his papers.

Du Sollier was succeeded by Jean Stiltingh (1703–62), the most distinguished scholar between

---

[1] Memoir in *Acta SS.*, t. v Augusti; it is by Stiltingh.

Papebroch and the Revolution.[1] Stiltingh was a
versatile and unusually rapid worker, with a capacity
for copious yet orderly composition. This phase of
the *Acta* is distinguished by the long historical
commentaries preceding the documents; this was a
fashion to which impetus had been given in the
July and August volumes by the occurrence of
St Ignatius Loyola and St Bernard of Clairvaux.
In his day—and it was the day of *philosophes* and
encyclopédistes—Stiltingh acquired a reputation every
whit as great as that of Papebroch, but in his hands
the commentary, which has inevitably aged with the
passage of time, showed an unfortunate tendency to
increase beyond bounds. Though dying at an age
which even then was young for a Bollandist, he filled
the best part of ten volumes of the *Acta* with what a
Bollandist of our own day has called his inexhaustible flood of learned improvisation.[2] Stiltingh's was
the last great name under the *ancien régime*. He was
followed as doyen by Constantine Suyskens[3] (1714–
1771), a scholar of the second rank, but one whom all
franciscanisants will remember for his *editio princeps*
of the *Legend of the Three Companions*. The last
senior was De Bye, not unworthy of his place, whose
fate it was to fight for long years to save a doomed
vessel.

The suppression of the Society of Jesus was the
end of a long process of struggle and intrigue. When
the blow fell in 1773 there were some who hoped to

[1] Memoir in *Acta SS.*, t. VI Augusti.
[2] 'Le flot intarissable de son improvisation érudite,' Peeters, *L'Œuvre
des Bollandistes*, p. 46.
[3] Memoir in *Acta SS.*, t. IV Octobris.

preserve the library and even the work of the Bollandists, while others looked forward only to acquiring their books. In the midst of plots and proposals the four remaining scholars continued their work, and volume IV of October appeared in 1780; from the title-page the letters S.J. were significantly missing. Meanwhile the remaining Bollandists had been transferred bag and baggage to the abbey of Caudenberg, within the walls of Brussels, which an Austrian governmental plan had designed as residuary legatee of the work. This abbey in its turn was suppressed by Joseph II, not before the unconquerable ship's company had sent volume V to press. Two years later a decree of government went forth that work on the *Acta* should come to an end, and the official mind had the graceful thought of fixing the date of demise for 1 November. Even this did not crush De Bye, and he was assisted by an endeavour on the part of the French Maurists to buy up the library and the literary rights. This aroused national jealousy in Belgium, and a scheme was set on foot to transfer proprietary rights to the Premonstratensian abbey of Tongerloo; the deal was carried through in August of the fateful year 1789. Two of the ex-Jesuits were still alive and able to act as instructors, and despite the outbreak of the Revolution, with all its repercussions in the Low Countries, and incredible as it may seem, volume VI of October was duly printed at Tongerloo in 1794. That was the end. In the same year the armies of the Convention flooded across Belgium bringing the Republic. A few books and papers were evacuated to Germany; others were hidden or perished. Bollandism, firing its cannon till the ports were flooded, went down at last.

During the forty years that followed, various schemes, some sinister, some burlesque, were devised both for salvaging the *Acta* and, alternatively, for picking up any of the cargo of the wreck that might have been washed up by the storms of the time. In the Europe established by the Congress of Vienna an independent Belgium had its place from 1830 onwards, and the decades after Waterloo saw a religious reaction throughout what had been the Napoleonic Empire. In 1814 the Society of Jesus was revived by Pius VII and a Belgian province was established in 1832. The work of reconstruction however was so vast that there was little occasion or inclination to exhume Bollandism, though parts of the old library and papers turned up here and there and some found their way into the Bibliothèque de Bourgogne, now the Royal Library at Brussels. In the event, the resurrection was due to a curious chance. A queer and incompetent society was founded in Paris for the purpose of hagiography, and negotiations were opened with the Belgian government to acquire the goodwill and some of the relics of the *Acta*. Once again patriotic susceptibilities were aroused, and the influential and far-sighted Rector of the University of Louvain, Mgr. de Ram, headed a petition that Bollandism should be revived and entrusted to the Belgian Jesuits. In 1837 a scratch team of three (later four) was installed in the Jesuit college at Brussels with a small government subvention, a few books and some library privileges, but without the tools and the still more precious traditions that their predecessors had accumulated. It is a striking witness to the strength of Flemish fibre and to the vitality of the ghost of Bollandism that from 1845 onwards the remaining October volumes of the *Acta* began to appear at short intervals. It is not surprising that they should on the whole have fallen short of the old standards; a group of inexperienced scholars had been set to produce the goods, and they did their best to oblige; the learned world of history, which in the 1840s was, save in Germany, largely a world of literary men, welcomed the revival. The difficulty was to find the men. Some withdrew; others, such as Antoine Tinnebroek and Edouard Carpentier,[1] died long before their time. The situation was saved by the emergence of a volcanic genius, Victor De Buck (1817–76).[2] De Buck was a man of intense vitality and versatility, endowed with a memory which Macaulay might have admired and a fearless rapidity of judgment. Despite the ceaseless, if not breathless, activity of the early years of the revival, he had amused himself by reading and annotating the existing fifty-three folios of the *Acta*. He had all Papebroch's courage and integrity, and if he lacked the master's maturity and poise he had a mind capable of intuitions and flashes of light that put him among the great. One of his achievements was to recognize that the so-called martyrology of

---

[1] For these, see Peeters, 'Après un siècle,' pp. xxiii, xxviii.
[2] For him, see article by P. V. Baesten in *Précis historiques*, xxv (1876), pp. 389–410.

St Jerome was a mosaic of calendars; another was his demolition of the current opinion, too often translated into liturgical practice, that the presence of a red-stained ampulla near a burial niche in the catacombs was a proof of martyrdom. This piece of criticism bade fair to win for De Buck a share in the fate as well as in the renown of Papebroch. His memoir had been a confidential one for the attention of authority, but there was a leak, and the author was indignantly attacked as an interested and insincere sceptic. De Buck made no attempt at a public defence in which he might have pressed home his point; this was nevertheless silently taken by the Roman authorities and has never since been questioned. Unlike the Bollandists of the past, De Buck was something of a celebrity in the Europe of the sixties. He was the friend of Dupanloup and Montalembert, and corresponded with the leaders of the Oxford movement and of the Orthodox party of reunion; he had his full share of the last infirmity of noble minds in Belgium—the conviction that he could understand the illogical English. In 1869–70 he was chosen by his general to serve as his theologian at the Vatican Council. De Buck worked upon the *Acta* for twenty-six years, and though never doyen of the group was in fact its heart and its motive power. In the words of Père Peeters, though he was not a typical leader of men his impetuous onset carried all before it and compelled the irresolute to take some kind of action, if only to save their skins. His last years, like those of Papebroch, were spent in blindness and malady.

De Buck's death in 1876 left Bollandism once more in danger. There was no master to take his place, and no firm tradition or settled policy had as yet been established. The methods of the past were being rapidly outmoded by the new critical school of Germany, while the editors of the *Monumenta Germaniae Historica* and the ex-pupils of the *École des Chartes* were setting a wholly new standard of excellence in the publication and criticism of medieval texts. The thirteenth and last volume of October, which appeared in 1883, some six years after De Buck's death, has been condemned as the poorest in the whole collection. The names on its title-page were all of men no longer living, and readers may well have thought that the enterprise had come to an end.

Already, however, the situation had been restored once more by the advent of a man of genius. This was Charles De Smedt (1831–1911), who was destined, though no longer young, to be for thirty-five years the *genius loci* and to effect a new creation, the Bollandism of our own time. De Smedt, though only thirty-odd years junior to De Buck, belonged altogether to the new world, the scientific and critical world of the nineteenth century. He realized that hagiography could no longer be a hit-or-miss affair, the work of industrious compilers and amateur historians illuminated by the occasional appearance of genius. The Bollandist must be a scholar trained in the new skills, disposing of all the new technical aids, and making for himself all the tools needful for his speciality. He must work to a plan wider than the needs of the next volume, a plan that should embrace every possible sphere and department of hagiography. Under De Smedt's guidance a whole series of reforms and new ventures was inaugurated. Texts were to be presented in accordance with the demands of modern criticism, after a complete assembly and classification of manuscripts, and with a full *apparatus criticus* that would satisfy the philologist as well as the higher critic. As a necessary preparation for this, lists were to be compiled of all hagiographical manuscripts in the libraries of the world, and catalogues established of all books, monographs and articles of a hagiographical character. Such departments of history as the Byzantine, Syriac, Slav and Celtic were to be assigned to individuals for intensive study. To encourage research and publication, to invite criticism and to guard against the Bollandists becoming scholars of the squirrel family, endlessly heaping up documents which might or might not be used by their distant successors, if not previously published by other scholars, a periodical, *Analecta Bollandiana*, was started in 1882 for the printing of texts and studies over the whole calendar of saints. This particular project rapidly proliferated. From being little more than an appendage of the *Acta*, and written in Latin, it took the shape of a modern review. Notices of books began to appear, and later a periodical review of all literature dealing with the saints.

De Smedt had the good fortune to be joined by a succession of men who in their varied abilities rivalled the giants of the past. There was Albert Poncelet

(1861–1912), a brilliant, tireless and methodical worker with a special interest in early medieval history; he was for many years the soul of the *Analecta*. There was François Van Ortroy (1854–1917), one of the most attractive figures of Bollandist history, impulsive, warm-hearted, witty, downright, with a face and figure worthy of the pencil of a Hogarth or a Caran d'Ache. Destined to compile the biography of St Carlo Borromeo, he spent years in Italy where he won the friendship of a living saint (the Milanese professor, Blessed Contardo Ferrini) and of a future pope (Pius XI), and was diverted to an interest in his patron of Assisi, recently popularized by Renan and Sabatier. Finally, and greatest of all, there was Hippolyte Delehaye (1859–1941), who resumed in his single person many of the characteristic qualities of the heroic age of the *Acta*. For a quarter of a century Delehaye was doyen of the group, and the Bollandist *par excellence*, and was hailed as such by the whole world of learning. Besides his work on the bibliographies, and what may be called his office work on the *Acta* and *Analecta*, Père Delehaye produced four classics of critical scholarship in his monumental edition of the Byzantine synaxary (1902), in his commentary on the martyrology of St Jerome (1931), in his study of the Roman legendary (1936) and in the commentary, compiled by himself and his colleagues, on the Roman martyrology (1940),[1] while he broke fresh ground by

[1] The various editions of the martyrologies may confuse a casual reader. The text of the vulgate version of the martyrology of Jerome was critically edited by Duchesne and de Rossi in 1894 for *Acta SS.*,

contributing to the *Subsidia Hagiographica* three short books, penetrating in judgment and perfect in form, that found a public far wider than that of the *Acta* or the *Analecta*: *Les légendes hagiographiques* (1905), *Les origines du culte des martyrs* (1912) and *Les passions des martyrs et les genres littéraires* (1921).

The thirty years from 1882 onwards were indeed the most fruitful and pacific period that Bollandism had known since the partnership of Bolland and Henskens. From a shifting group of editors it had become, without losing anything of its intimate character, one of the institutions of the learned world of Europe. A fortunate accident of town-planning had meanwhile (1905) compelled a move from the cramped quarters of the city to spacious new buildings in the suburbs on a site designated by King Leopold II. The work of De Smedt and his colleagues had come to maturity, and there was hope of a steady production of the volumes of November.

Once more, however, a deadly blow fell, though this time through agencies entirely external. The invasion of Belgium by the Germans and the subsequent occupation (1914–18) paralysed work and cut the Bollandists off from all friendly intercourse with scholars. Recruitment was impossible; Van

---

t. II i Novembris. The martyrology itself was dismembered and reconstructed critically by Delehaye, and published (text by Dom H. Quentin, commentary by H. Delehaye) in 1931 as t. II ii Novembris. The commentary on the Roman martyrology, to which all the Bollandists of the day under Delehaye's leadership contributed, is the introductory volume to December, and appeared in 1940.

Ortroy died in 1917 and Delehaye, in common with many Belgian clerics, took a considerable part in anti-German propaganda and intelligence. He was arrested and fined in 1916, and when, with a contemptuous disregard of the German police, he continued his activities, he was again arrested and after an imprisonment of three months was tried on a capital charge, from which he escaped with a long sentence of hard labour. His confinement ceased shortly before the Armistice, but when he returned to the Boulevard Saint-Michel Bollandism was again almost extinct. Undismayed, he gathered his colleagues round him once more, the Bollandists of yesterday and today, and in 1925 he was able to publish volume IV of November. The two decades between the Wars were a time of harvest as well as cultivation, and Delehaye had the satisfaction of completing, with the assistance of his colleagues, the great commentary on the Roman martyrology, which appeared as the introductory volume (or *Propylaeum*) to December. It was dispatched to press in May 1940, only three days before the second German invasion of Belgium. Delehaye lived to see disaster once more threaten his work, and died while his country was once again severed from part at least of the Western world, but this time Belgium suffered less than many of the other countries overrun by the German armies; the *Analecta* remained in production, and Bollandism since 1945 has continued firmly to maintain the position that it first attained sixty years ago.

With Delehaye we have reached our own times, but before concluding two more Bollandists may be mentioned. The first is Paul Peeters (1870–1950), a scholar of mingled French and Belgian ancestry. Peeters, who as a young man was a brilliant classic and humanist, early showed himself endowed with the gift of tongues and turned to the East, where he proceeded from Arabic and Syriac to Coptic and Armenian and the still more unfamiliar Georgian. His life-work was to add the confines of oriental Christianity to Bollandism, and to resolve the many problems of literary parentage and provenance that surround the records of the native saints. Besides a ceaseless output of texts and studies, Peeters added a third great bibliography, the *Bibliotheca hagiographica orientalis*, to the Bollandist family, and established himself as one of the most notable orientalists in western Europe. It is for the specialist to appreciate and for the profane to admire such work. Père Peeters, however, the life-long admirer of Saint-Simon and Sainte-Beuve, remained always a humanist, a stylist and a keen and sympathetic observer of men. It is to him that we are beholden, not only for an exquisitely balanced account of Bollandism presented in racy and idiomatic language, but also for a gallery of portraits of his confrères which, besides their value as documents in the history of scholarship, are masterpieces of delicate observation conveyed with an urbanity and sureness of touch which place them high among examples of the genre in modern French literature. In his turn Père Peeters received the meed of praise in the *Analecta*, though from a pen less golden and less airily poised than his own.

Secondly and lastly, I would mention a living Bollandist, who learnt a part of his trade at the feet of R. L. Poole at Oxford, and whom we are honoured to reckon among our Corresponding Fellows. Père Paul Grosjean has long made Britannia his province, but his peculiar domain is with the multitudinous saints of the Britons and Bretons of the west, and in the twilight of Cymru and Eire. Even while we speak of him he may be pursuing the elusive Gildas or watching with Pangur Bán the darting mice of the *Hisperica Famina*.

Those who have followed the long story of the Bollandists may pause at the end to assemble their reflections. The most remarkable feature of the Society would seem to be its obstinate survival as a recognizable and active agency of scholarship that has kept its identity unchanged, and has again and again been blessed in a crisis by the uncovenanted gift of genius. There is indeed nothing in the learned world quite like it. The only other small and 'immortal' group at all comparable is the knot of French scholars, who, after two and a half centuries, have carried down the history of French literature almost to the age of Villon. They, however, differ in many ways from the Bollandists. They are neither the descendants nor the heirs, but only the continuators, of the Maurists who began the project. They are not scholars who have been initiated in their task by slow degrees, but experts who have been chosen precisely by reason of their competence in a particular field. And, finally, that field is itself a specialized one; they do not have to cover the whole world and the whole Christian era. The Bollandists on the other hand have never been more than six strong, and their numbers for long periods have stood at four or three. Setting aside mere birds of passage or extraneous assistants, there cannot have been, all told, more than sixty or seventy Bollandists *de métier*. An undertaking that hangs on the destinies of four or five men would seem a bad risk for the actuaries, yet again and again the dying flame has found new fuel and once, when extinguished, was rekindled to burn more brightly than before. It has never been saved by a *coup d'état* or a massive transfusion of blood.

The second reflection will perhaps be that Bollandists from first to last have borne something of a family resemblance. They have all sprung from that mingled stock that for centuries has populated the citied region between Rhine and Aisne—a stock of which part is gifted beyond the ordinary with industry and perseverance, while another part inherits the clarity of France and the sun of Burgundy. It is a region that from the days of Erasmus and Latomus to those of Cumont and Pirenne has produced a succession of great scholars and humanists. The Bollandists have all been disciplined by the firm classical culture upon which has been grafted the tradition of French letters. They have all passed through the Jesuit noviciate and clericate and theologate with its years of teaching, and finally all have by long habit acquired the final family likeness of the Museum

Bollandianum. Of all these influences perhaps the
one that has kept the Bollandists firm at their post
and faithful to their ideal has been the Jesuit dedica-
tion and the conviction that their work, the attainment and presentation of one facet of the truth and
beauty of the heavenly Jerusalem, is essentially worth
all the pains it may cost.

And finally, what is the future of Bollandism?
The open road, at least, will always stretch before
them. The race of the saints will never become
extinct, and when the Bollandists of the twenty-first
century have reached St Silvester—not an inappro-
priate *revenant* to meet our unborn Papebroch at the
close of the Bollandist cycle—January will open up
its all-but-virgin pages once more. Can half a dozen
individuals drawn from the provinces of a single
nation within a single religious order cope with a
task growing ever more vast, in a world where
historical undertakings of far less magnitude occupy
the energies of a whole institute with a regiment of
typists? Doubtless the Society of Jesus, if put to it,
could lay on, as they say, an institute that would not
disgrace Ann Arbor or Dumbarton Oaks, but it
would no longer be the Museum Bollandianum.
And then, are not others now doing the work? The
religious orders, the Catholic universities, medievalists and byzantinists throughout the world are
publishing lives of the saints in abundance. How
can the Bollandists survive? And are there not
problems, other than the purely technical and
critical, that await the hagiographer of today and
tomorrow? Must he not examine the frontiers of

natural and supernatural activity, and delimit the functions of the psychologist and of the mystical theologian?

We may ask these questions, but we cannot answer them, and as historians we need not try to do so. We may be allowed to end with the Vergilian wish: *stet fortuna domus, et avi numerentur avorum.*

The Maurists

There is no adequate and critical modern history of the Maurists. Dom P. Denis, who hoped to write one, contributed valuable articles to the early numbers of the *Revue Mabillon* (then devoted largely to Maurist history), but did not live to fulfil his promise. The fundamental literary sources are those of the Maurists themselves, some of which have only been printed in recent years: Dom E. Martène, *Histoire de la Congrégation de Saint-Maur*, ed. Dom G. Charvin (9 vols., Ligugé 1928–43); the same writer's *La vie des justes*, ed. Dom B. Heurtebize (3vols., Ligugé 1924–6); the *Nécrologe . . . de Saint-Germain-des-Prés*, ed. J. B. Varel (Paris 1896); Dom P. Tassin, *Histoire littéraire de la congrégation de Saint-Maur* (Brussels 1770), completed by U. Robert (Paris 1881) and U. Berlière and H. Wilhelm (Paris 1908). The vivid studies by E. de Broglie of Mabillon and Montfaucon (see below) are selective, though scholarly (Paris 1888, 1891); the account by Dom P. Schmitz in his *Histoire de l'Ordre de Saint Benoît*, v (Maredsous 1949), pp. 266–77, is short. For manageable lists of Maurist writings, see article 'Maurists' in *Catholic Encyclopedia* and 'Mauristes' in *Dictionnaire de théologie catholique* and (less manageable) *Dictionnaire d'archéologie chrétienne et de liturgie*. Dom H. Leclercq has much relevant material in *Mabillon* (2 vols., Paris 1953–7).

2

The Maurists

A YEAR ago our theme was the work of the
Bollandists. Their name suggests immediately,
to all acquainted with European historiography, the
name of another body of religious, many of them
the contemporaries of Henskens and Papebroch, and
it would be impossible to omit from even the shortest
list of great historical enterprises the achievement of
the Maurists. The two bodies of men and their work,
nevertheless, have little in common save an equal
devotion to accurate scholarship. What impresses us
in the history of Bollandism is its continuity of spirit
and undeviating aim over more than three hundred
years, during which a very small but perpetually self-
renewing group has pursued a single narrowly defined
task, which is still far from completion. With the
Maurists, on the other hand, it is the magnitude,
the variety and the high quality of the achievement
that strikes the imagination. While the Bollandists,
a small family in a single house, have in three
centuries produced in major work no more than a
row of sixty-seven folios, the Maurists, in a little
more than a hundred years, published matter enough
to stock a small library, and left behind them letters,
papers and transcripts which have been used and
exploited by scholars for nearly two centuries since.
Indeed, it would be both impossible and alien to the

scope of our interests to attempt the briefest survey
of Maurist scholarship in its entirety, and my remarks
today will be confined to their publications on
European history after the decline of the Roman
Empire. Who were the Maurists, and wherein lay
their peculiar excellence?

The Maurists, to give them their proper style,
were Benedictine monks of the Congregation of
St Maurus. Their origin was as follows.[1] The wars
of religion and of the League had overtaken the
monastic order in France before it had been able to
profit by the reforming spirit of the Council of Trent
and the Counter-Reformation. When peace and order
returned to France many of the abbeys were desolate,
others were decadent, and in many of the greatest
and wealthiest the system of commendatory abbots
remained as a legacy from the Middle Ages. The
early years of the seventeenth century, however, saw
a great revival of spiritual life in France.[2] It was the
epoch in which all that was best in Spanish and
Italian piety crossed the Alps and the Pyrenees, and
in which a flowering of French sanctity and genius,
and a spirit of union in well-doing, gave a new life
to the Church, before the bitter and blighting wind
of religious discord and political rivalry soured the
spring's bright promise of sunshine and fruit. In
every region and institute new life stirred, and the
great political churchmen of the age, the cardinals
La Rochefoucauld and Richelieu, gave help in their

[1] cf. P. Schmitz, *Histoire de l'Ordre de S. Benoît*, IV (1948), pp. 21–52.
[2] The best account of this is in H. Bremond, *Histoire littéraire du
sentiment religieux en France*, III, 'La conquête mystique' (Paris 1921).

own ways and measures. One of the reforming decrees of Trent had ordered the formation in each province or region of a monastic congregation, that is, a confederation of neighbouring houses bound together by a single code under an organized authority and system of discipline. One such group was initiated in 1600 in the monastery of Saint-Vanne at Verdun by a saintly reformer, Dom Didier de la Cour (1550–1623); it flourished greatly and soon counted numerous houses in its federation. Lorraine was not at that time part of the kingdom of France, but the reform soon spread across the frontier and even reached Paris. Here political difficulties quickly arose, and it was decided to form a separate congregation of the French houses; this was achieved in 1618, and the new federation took as its patron St Maurus, the disciple of St Benedict who, as the early legend ran, had brought the Rule and the spirit of the patriarch of Western monachism to the monastery of Fleury-sur-Loire.

One of the principal aims of all Benedictine reforms since the early fifteenth century had been the replacement of the outmoded copying of manuscripts and compilation of chronicles and encyclopedias by learned work based on the humanist education and the critical methods of the Renaissance. The congregation of Saint-Vanne had given a large place in its legislation to the fostering of studies and learning, and this ideal had been part of the legacy inherited by the younger Maurist body. That the daughter succeeded in eclipsing her mother so notably in this respect was due to a number of coincident advantages: the spirit of the age in France, the appearance of a great legislator followed by a succession of scholars of genius, and the acquisition of headquarters in the capital at a moment when Paris became, for the second time in her long history, the intellectual centre of Europe.

The seventeenth century, or more exactly the period from about 1630 to 1730, was a golden age of scholarship. The great and absorbing theological controversies of the Reformation, in which almost all the great minds of the age had been engaged, were now near spent, and a period of relative peacefulness began; throughout Europe a generation of highly educated and civilized men, full of curiosity and appreciation of the history and writings of the distant past, was able to review the treasures, printed and unprinted, that had been assembled in the great libraries and collections of Europe.[1] The spirit of the age, which witnessed so many triumphs of mathematical discovery and the first great advances in natural science, showed itself in the humane disciplines as an influence in the direction of criticism and analysis. Moreover, there appeared on every side in France an outpouring of genius comparable to that which had been seen in Italy in the fifteenth, and in Spain in the sixteenth century.

The congregation of Saint-Maur was fortunate, soon after its beginnings, to have as its superior-general Dom Grégoire Tarrisse (1575–1648), an ex-soldier and administrator who became a monk

---

[1] For this movement in England, see D. C. Douglas, *The English Scholars* (2nd ed., London 1951).

at the age of forty-nine and soon rose to high office,
largely owing to the discerning patronage of Richelieu.[1] He revised its constitutions, transferred its
headquarters to the ancient abbey of Saint-Germain-
des-Prés, and used all his abilities and energies to
make learned work the distinguishing employment
of its monks. In this he was aided by the organization of the congregation. The traditional Benedictine
monastery has always been a fully autonomous abbey,
ruled by an abbot elected for life. This system in the
later Middle Ages had proved resistant to reform,
and matters had been rendered still worse by the
prevalent abuse of commendatory abbots, by which
the monks were deprived at once of most of their
revenues and of their rightful head. Many of the
reforming congregations had endeavoured to avoid
these ills by giving supreme power to a general
chapter or a superior-general, and even (as in the
case of Saint-Maur) by making the congregation,
not the individual monastery, the unit to which a
monk belonged by profession, and within which he
could be moved about at will by his superiors. This
reduced the commendatory abbots, who still existed
in considerable numbers, from a position of control
to one of patronage only. Dom Tarrisse had thus a
free field in which to develop his programme. The

[1] For Mabillon's appreciation of Dom Tarrisse, see preface to *Annales
O.S.B.*, VI. cf. F. Rousseau, *Un promoteur de l'érudition française béné-
dictine: Dom Grégoire Tarrisse* (Bruges 1924), and H. Stein, 'Le premier
Supérieur général de la Congrégation de Saint-Maur: Dom Grégoire
Tarrisse,' in *Mélanges [et documents . . . de Mabillon]* (Paris 1908),
pp. 49–89. cf. also E. Bishop, 'Richelieu and the Maurists,' in *Downside
Review*, XXX (1911), pp. 271–90, reprinted in *Liturgica Historica* (Oxford
1918), pp. 462–74.

two essential features were an exceptionally long
course of studies, including besides philosophy and
theology a thorough grounding in the classics and a
thorough study of church history, and a centraliza-
tion of talent at the Paris house. While intellectual
ability was not, and could not be, even with the
Maurists, a *sine qua non* of admission to the habit,
the knowledge that a severe course of study must be
traversed, and that mental work of one kind or
another was the approved pursuit of the body, must
have tended to direct talent towards their houses.
Once a monk's long training was completed, his local
superior was instructed to do his best to direct his
subject's interest towards some aspect of patristic or
historical work. If after a few years he showed
unusual promise, he might hope to be sent to
Saint-Germain-des-Prés. There and throughout the
congregation, a policy of library-building was adopted; a careful list was drawn up of the essential
books, and further purchases were made to meet
the needs of the individuals. The library of Saint-
Germain itself, which inherited the manuscript treasures of Corbie, soon came to be one of the best
equipped in Europe, and the monks had in addition
facilities to visit and even to borrow from the Royal
Library and Colbert's library and the many rich
and private collections of Paris.

But though encouraged and directed, Maurist
studies were in early days never rigidly blueprinted
and organized. There was nothing of the institute,
the team or even the seminar, at Saint-Germain in
the seventeenth century. The great works were in

general, and especially in the lifetime of Mabillon, conceived and executed by a single scholar, who in time selected one or two younger colleagues to help and perhaps to succeed him. When once a project had been approved and was under way, however, a scholar could draw upon his community, and even upon the whole congregation, for assistance in copying manuscripts, reading proofs, indexing and the like, but there was never a 'director' of research or publication, nor was the whole congregation a 'learned body.' It would seem impossible to estimate the numbers of those actually engaged upon literary work. The whole congregation held between three and four thousand monks, and a contemporary put the number of scholars at forty,[1] but this, if at all accurate, can only have included those actually engaged as principals in producing published work; the number of those engaged directly or indirectly in technical assistance, the collection of materials and private study must have been considerably greater. Nevertheless, even if the number of scholars is put at a couple of hundred and the total number of monks at three thousand, the percentage is still a very low one.

Besides books and manuscripts, the Maurists had three sources of assistance characteristic of their age: conversation, correspondence and foreign travel. The

---

[1] Nicole (cited by Leclercq, *Mabillon*, p. 566, from Bremond, *L'Abbé Tempête*, p. 183) wrote: 'Il n'y a pas quarante religieux dans la congrégation [de quatre mille] qui fassent une vie d'étude.' This would seem to be the source of Leclercq's own statement (*Mabillon*, p. 545): 'les Mauristes comptaient une quarantaine de savants sur un total de trois [*sic*] mille religieux environ.'

4

learned reunion, the *conversazione*, was an essential
feature of life at Saint-Germain. For almost a century, from the rise of Luc d'Achery to the death of
Bernard de Montfaucon, the abbey was the scene of
regular weekly gatherings of all the scholarship and
much of the connoisseurship of Paris and France.[1]
Either in the spacious cell of d'Achery in the infir-
mary, or in the garden of the abbey, or later on the
road to Suresnes and its *déjeuners*, projects were
discussed, information exchanged, and all the latest
discoveries and books aired for criticism. While
Du Cange and Baluze debated with d'Achery and
Mabillon, the young Michel Germain and Thierry
Ruinart could listen and learn. The brilliance of these
gatherings, the galaxy of talent and power to
be found among the visitors to Saint-Germain—
Hérouval, Bignon, Fleury, Bossuet and Fénelon;
Le Tellier, Colbert, the archbishop of Reims, Le
Tellier's son, the Abbé Louvois, son of the minister,
the cardinals de Bouillon and de Coislin, the duc
d'Aumont and the duc de Chevreuse—all these,
and many more, have been preserved for us in the
correspondence of the abbey, as they are preserved in
the Memoirs of Saint-Simon and the pages of
Emmanuel de Broglie.

Thirdly, there were the *voyages littéraires*, the
long expeditions across France or Europe in search
of manuscripts to copy, books to buy and antiquities
to visit. Here, as we saw on an earlier page, Henskens and

---

[1] The *locus classicus* is E. de Broglie, *Mabillon et la Société de l'Abbaye de Saint-Germain-des-Prés à la fin du dix-septième siècle* (2 vols., Paris 1888), I, pp. 52ff.

Papebroch were first in the field, but the journeys of Mabillon and his younger companions, and those of Martène and Durand, are more familiar owing to the literary record left by Mabillon himself, to the voluminous correspondence between the travellers and their friends, and to the descriptions and drawings of monuments and architecture that have been preserved.[1]

It would be quite impossible to give in a few pages even an outline of the historical work of the Maurists, and a catalogue of books and names would be both useless and tedious. Altogether, the Maurists were 'in production' for a century and a half (*c.* 1640–1789), and four phases can be seen in their work. The first, from 1640 to 1665, is the pre-Mabillon period of individual and undirected effort, in which the single great figure of d'Achery slowly emerges to propose methods and a programme. The second period, from 1665 to 1707, is the age of Mabillon, in which his own works and those of his disciples and companions fill the foreground. The third phase, from 1708 to 1741, is dominated by the two eminent scholars Martène and Montfaucon. The fourth, from 1742 to the end, is the age of the *epigoni*, the lesser men. Within the periods, the character of the work shows a gradual evolution. In the first, it is sporadic and individual; a history here, an edition there, a series of collections of texts. In the second, we can see the programme of Tarrisse and d'Achery

---

[1] Mabillon described the German tour in *Vetera Analecta*, IV, pp. 3ff., 'Iter Germanicum,' and the Italian experience in *Iter Italicum* (1687). Both E. de Broglie and H. Leclercq give full accounts.

unfolding in the work of Mabillon and his immediate associates; this is the era also of the editions of the Latin Fathers. In the third, the Greek Fathers are edited under Montfaucon, and Martène is working on liturgy. This third period merges into the fourth, which is the period of large-scale works and series on the one hand, and of numberless regional and civic histories on the other.

If Dom Tarrisse was the originator of the Maurist idea, the man to embody it in work done and in plans laid down was Dom Luc d'Achery (1609–85). It was he who, as counsellor to the superior-general, outlined the programme of patristic texts and historical collections that formed the germ of the Maurist achievement; it was he who, as librarian, built up the magnificent collection of books and allowed the Sunday afternoon reunions of scholars to develop in his room, and it was he who chose, received and taught Mabillon.

The programme devised by Tarrisse and d'Achery had three divisions: first, a general history of the monastic order, culminating in a history of the Maurist congregation; secondly, a collection of the lives of monastic saints; and thirdly, new editions of the monastic writers of the Middle Ages. All these objects were attained in great part by the *Acta Sanctorum O.S.B.*, the *Annales O.S.B.*, the *Histoire littéraire* of the Maurist congregation itself, the many histories of individual monasteries and the editions of Bernard and others. In a later generation, as we have seen, the plan proliferated: lives of the early martyrs and others were added to those of monks;

texts of the Fathers, Greek and Latin, were undertaken; a series of auxiliary disciplines were charted;
a number of 'aids' for historians were compiled; and
the latest Maurists began to conceive the whole past
of France as their province.

When Mabillon joined d'Achery in 1664 a great
quantity of material had already been assembled at
Saint-Germain. Admirable as were the industry and
perspicacity of d'Achery and his new lieutenant, the
preparatory work of collection had already been
largely accomplished. Had this not been so, the
achievement of Mabillon in his first years at the
abbey, prodigious as it was, would have been quite
impossible. As things were, a steady stream of folios
soon began to flow.

Mabillon stands by himself in a class apart in the
history of Maurist scholarship, and even the shortest
account must contain a sketch of his life and work.[1]
Born of humble country stock in Champagne in 1632,
and clothed a monk of Saint-Remi of Reims, he was
sent to several houses in poor health before attracting
the attention of d'Achery while at Saint-Denis. He
became a member of the community of Saint-
Germain in 1664 and within a few months took the
place of d'Achery's lieutenant, Claude Chantelou,
recently dead. Within four years he had shown his

---

[1] For Mabillon, the essential books are: Dom T. Ruinart, *Abrégé de la
vie de Dom Jean Mabillon* (Paris 1709; Latin translation, Padua 1714;
reprint of French life as *Mabillon*, Maredsous 1933); E. de Broglie,
Mabillon (see introductory note p. 34); above all, H. Leclercq, art.
'Mabillon' in *D.A.C* and *Mabillon* (above, note p. 34). For a short sketch,
see M. D. Knowles, 'Jean Mabillon,' *Journal of Ecclesiastical History*,
X, 2 (1959), pp. 153–73; reprinted in M. D. Knowles, *The Historian and
Character* (1963).

mettle with an edition, for which much of the preparatory work had been done by others, of the works
of St Bernard, which he adorned with notes and
introductory notices. This edition in its revised form
(1690) became, and still remains, the standard edition,
though it is on the point of being superseded by that
of Dom Jean Leclercq. Concurrently with the work
on St Bernard, Mabillon had been assisting d'Achery
in the production of a series of volumes containing
lives of the monastic saints arranged chronologically;
six appeared between 1668 and 1680. These were
much more than a series of texts; Mabillon contributed prefaces and a series of excursus to each;
in the former he reviewed what would now be called
the spirituality of the period concerned, in the latter
he selected difficult or controversial points of monastic
and liturgical history and dealt with them critically
and magisterially. These works were received with
enthusiasm by the learned world of Europe, and it
was realized that a new star of considerable magnitude had appeared in the firmament. It was not,
however, till 1681 that he showed his true quality
of genius. The work which appeared in that year,
the *De Re Diplomatica*, which is generally regarded
as its author's masterpiece, was, like many another
masterpiece, an 'occasional' work, the outcome of a
challenge.[1] When Mabillon was a young man, diplomatic—the science, that is, of criticizing manuscript
charters and official letters and documents of all
kinds—did not exist. Hitherto every controversial

---

[1] The best analysis of *De Re Diplomatica* is that of L. Levillain in
Mélanges, pp. 195–252.

point had been tackled in isolation, but in 1675 the
great Bollandist scholar, Daniel Papebroch, had
taken a step forward. In the *Propylaeum* or introduction to the second volume of April saints he had
propounded a number of rules for discriminating
between genuine and spurious charters, and had
condemned as spurious a series of early monastic
charters of Saint-Denis and Corbie. Mabillon saw
that the authenticity of a whole class of documents
was at stake, and resolved to extract from all the
charters and diplomas of which he had knowledge
their characteristics of writing, style, form, dating,
signature, sealing and the rest, and to propound
thence rules for the authentication of various types
of record. In less than six years, and without aban-
doning his other commitments, he had done his work,
and it is the measure of his learning and his genius
that the first major work on diplomatic was definitive
on its subject. Methodically and patiently, with
admirable lucidity and economy, Mabillon proceeded
over the whole field of palaeography, linguistics,
chronology, sphragistics and the rest, providing
abundant examples and facsimiles, and passing with
ease from the broadest principles to the smallest
detail.

It is a testimony not only to the genius of the
writer but to the society of his times that the work
gave almost instant fame to its author throughout
Europe, and a fame not only among fellow scholars
but among all educated men—the kind of fame that
in different disciplines and centuries has been
attained by a Galileo and an Einstein. In truth the

De Re Diplomatica had not only created a discipline but had provided adepts with a textbook which was not ousted for almost two centuries, and then only by works which embodied its spirit and much of its detail. Mabillon, both then and thereafter, made errors of detail, but by and large his own rules should have served to prevent his lapses. He was weakest, perhaps, in philology and in some of the material details of palaeography. But his confrères, who produced a revised (but in many ways less satisfactory) third edition of his work were justified in writing: 'His system is true, and whoever would build on foundations other than his, will build on sand.' Papebroch, in a justly celebrated exchange of letters, accepted his conclusions and begged to be considered his pupil, and the great palaeographers of the past century, Sickel, Tangl, Giry, Delisle and Traube, have continued to proclaim his eminence.[1]

We cannot here follow Mabillon on his journeys, nor trace the great controversies, such as those with Armand de Rancé and with the opponents of the Benedictine edition of Augustine, in which he became engaged. Two further achievements must, however, be mentioned. The one is his pioneer work on Gallican and Roman liturgy, which had its source in the discoveries, including those of the Luxeuil lectionary and the Bobbio missal, made on his travels, and which was published in the treatise *De liturgia gallica* (1685) and in the texts and studies

---

[1] The words of L. Traube may be taken as representative (*Vorlesungen*, ed. P. Lehmann (Munich 1909), I, p. 22): 'So sehr ist darin alles monumental und nicht für den Augenblick, sondern für die Unsterblichkeit geschrieben.'

of his *Museum Italicum* (1687, 1689), which in the judgment of liturgists of today set him in the very front rank of their predecessors[1]; the other is the *Annales O.S.B.*, which contain his ripest reflections and are, in the realm of 'straight' history, his greatest work. In them he wrote the narrative of monastic history from St Benedict to the death of St Bernard, based directly on the literary and charter material with which he was so familiar, while to each volume he prefixed a long introduction giving a survey of the period and its characteristics. Mabillon commanded a Latin style of great lucidity and flexibility; he had an appreciation of the greatness and melancholy of human things and a sense, rare in his age, of the development of institutions and of the movement of cause and effect. In consequence, these introductions still retain their power to move the imagination and enlighten the mind.

Mabillon died on 27 December 1707, in his seventy-sixth year. He died, as he had lived, a simple monk surrounded by his brethren, and his resting-place was marked by a stone recording no more than name and date. He had refused a comfortable abbacy some years previously, and had come near receiving the cardinal's hat from his friend, Clement XII. His devoted pupil and companion, Thierry Ruinart, wrote almost immediately a short and intimate account of his life, dwelling particularly on the events of his last days. It is the

[1] cf. H. Leclercq in *D.A.C*, x (i), pp. 529–30: 'Il n'avait pas eu de devancier dans cette œuvre [sur l'office gallican] et on peut dire qu'il n'a pas eu d'imitateur.' But had Leclercq forgotten Edmund Bishop?

work of an affectionate admirer, but all that we
know of Mabillon from his writings and recorded
acts confirms the picture given by his friend.
Mabillon, indeed, stands next to the Venerable
Bede, whom he resembles so closely in mind and
character, as an embodiment of the ideal monk-
scholar, whose type has reappeared, recognizable
if less perfectly chiselled, in numberless figures from
Alcuin and Aelfric to Dom André Wilmart and
Dom Ursmer Berlière. In distinction of mind, in
humanity of outlook, in critical acumen and in
intellectual power he was acknowledged as pre-
eminent in an age of great men, and the judgment
of Coulton, that he remains the greatest monastic
historian,[1] will not easily be gainsaid by anyone
who considers the whole field of the European past.
Above and beyond his great qualities of critical
vision, and his truly phenomenal industry which
was so admirably focused on the appointed task, he
had a sobriety and warmth of feeling, a moderation,
a selflessness and a charity, that carried him above
the sphere of scholarship into the company of good
men who are loved as greatly as they are admired.
Unassuming, gentle and lovable as he certainly was,
Mabillon was severe and austere with himself, an
undaunted seeker after truth and an upholder of
principle in word and in work; if he loved peace
and ensued it he was also prepared to resist aggres-
sion and falsehood. The Maurists were fortunate,

[1] *Five Centuries of Religion* (Cambridge 1921), I, p. 3: 'There is no
monastic historian who for learning and impartiality comes even into
the same class as Mabillon.'

in their own day and ever since, to have had such a champion and representative of their ideal.

With the death of Mabillon, followed so soon by that of his gifted disciple Ruinart, what was in many ways the most illustrious period of Maurist scholarship came to an end. It was succeeded by what may be called the age of Martène and Montfaucon (d. 1741). Martène (1654–1739), 'le bon Emond' of Mabillon's letters, who died an octogenarian in 1739, was in many ways a survivor from another age.[1] His name is familiar to medievalists as the editor of two large collections of texts, the *Thesaurus novus anecdotorum* (5 vols., 1717) and the *Veterum scriptorum amplissima collectio* (9 vols., 1724–33). Like Mabillon and his two other disciples, Michel Germain and Thierry Ruinart, he was a monk of Saint-Remi of Reims. On his arrival at Saint-Germain he became the enthusiastic admirer and disciple of the then prior, Dom Claude Martin, son of Marie de l'Incarnation and one of the most saintly of the Maurists.[1] The attraction of Dom Claude was stronger than that of Mabillon, and Dom Edmond, after giving a measure of his quality by his *Commentary* on the Rule and his important *De antiquis monachorum ritibus*, followed his hero to Marmoutier in 1690 and, when Dom Claude died soon after, became his biographer in a saint's life which was published without permission; he was in consequence

[1] For Martène, see art. by H. Leclercq in *D.A.C.*
[1] For Dom Martin, see Dom E. Martène, *Histoire de la Congrégation de Saint-Maur*, VII, pp. 131–58, and H. Bremond, *Histoire littéraire du sentiment religieux en France*, VI (Paris 1922), pp. 177–226.

sent in disgrace to a period of penance. Mabillon
remained his friend, but for some reason Martène
declined his invitation to return and help with
the *Annals*. After Mabillon's death, however,
followed shortly by that of Ruinart, 'le saint homme
Emond' made amends to the dead by preparing the
final volume for the press. He had also become the
author of what is still the authoritative *Histoire de la
Congrégation de Saint-Maur*.

Dom Bernard Montfaucon (1655–1741) was of a
different stamp.[1] By birth and temper an aristocrat,
he had worn the sword for a short space before taking
the habit, and as a young man at Saint-Germain had
from the first taken another path to that of Mabillon
and had become the indefatigable editor of the Greek
Fathers, dealing in succession with Athanasius,
Origen and St John Chrysostom during a period of
fifty years, punctuated by a quadrennium as procurator in the Curia in succession to Claude Estiennot,
a position in which he was the loyal advocate and
adviser of Mabillon, then in the throes of a controversy on Augustine. After Mabillon's death Montfaucon succeeded him, both within the abbey, in
Paris and throughout the learned world, as the centre
and chief ornament of Maurist erudition. Though
always irreproachable as a priest and religious, Montfaucon was a degree nearer than Mabillon to being
a man of the world. Vivacious, high spirited and of
commanding presence, he was the host and leader of
a group more wordly and free of thought and speech

[1] For Montfaucon, see E. de Broglie, *Bernard de Montfaucon et les
Bernardins* (2 vols., Paris 1891).

than Du Cange and Baluze, and study and social
tasks broke in upon the solitude and observance of
the later Maurists. Montfaucon was perhaps the most
widely erudite of all his tribe. Besides his editions,
he created, in his *Paléographie grecque*, a new discipline to put beside the medieval palaeography of
Mabillon, and the work remained till very recent
times the essential textbook. He followed these by
two works of less permanent value which nevertheless
contained a vast amount of erudite information and
anticipated, by more than a century, the social and
art history of modern times; these were *Antiquité
expliquée* in fifteen volumes—a survey of the ancient
civilizations and their remains—and the unfinished
Monuments de la monarchie française (five volumes),
which aimed at being an illustrated introduction to
the artistic and social life of early France. Finally,
now a very old man, Montfaucon produced in 1739,
in two folio volumes, a catalogue of the manuscript
collections in the whole of Europe of which he had
taken notes for forty years, the *Bibliotheca biblio-
thecarum*.

Montfaucon was the last great Maurist. Already
the titles of two of his later works, which won him
such attention in his old age, reflects a change of outlook from that of Dom Tarrisse and Luc d'Achery.
They have no kind of religious purpose, and they
give an impression of a love of erudition and information for its own sake which is absent from all
Mabillon's work. Montfaucon and Martène were
indeed the last of the great age, and the former
was also the harbinger of a new epoch. Even before

their death the sunlight had faded and a cold wind
was springing up. Even though the warning light
had been showing long before the death of Louis XIV,
the catastrophe of the French church in the mid-
eighteenth century must always startle and confuse
one who has watched the splendours of revival only
a century before, with its galaxy of saints and great
men. When the great men departed with the *Grand
Monarque* the high controversies lost their stature
and spiritual warmth departed. The Maurists, like
all other bodies, were rent by Jansenism, Gallicanism,
and, as the century wore on, rationalism; and secu-
larism invaded the cloister. Nevertheless, their work
went on till the end, and much of it was technically
of a very high quality, though much of it was also the
collection of information on every kind of historical
subject rather than research and publication of matter
that was specifically monastic or ecclesiastical.

The last period is marked by the inception of
several large-scale projects, none of which was in
fact completed, and which were either 'wished on'
the Maurists or undertaken by them with at least
some encouragement from the publishers and book-
sellers.

The first in date was the *Gallia Christiana*. A
book with this title, the work of Claude Robert,
had appeared in 1626, and an enlarged and revised
version, by several members of the Sainte-Marthe
family, was published in 1656. The original intention
was to provide a list of the occupants of all the sees
of (modern) France from the earliest times, but the
project gradually broadened, as such projects will, to

include abbots and diocesan dignitaries. In 1710 the assembly of the French clergy had petitioned the superiors of the Maurists to undertake a new and more complete work, which should be an account of all the dioceses and abbeys of the country with lists and biographies of all office-holders. The request was granted, and to avoid controversies and jealousies it was decided to proceed alphabetically through the provinces, beginning with Aix. The monks deputed for the project got down to work, and between 1716 and 1785 thirteen great volumes appeared and the province of Trèves had been reached. Still indispensable as a work of reference, *faute de mieux*, the *Gallia* enshrines accounts of individual abbeys by some of the most eminent Maurists.

Alongside of the *Gallia*, another enormous scheme was implemented in 1721. This was a reflotation of a vast project of *Historiae Francorum scriptores* launched by André du Chesne in 1636, which had foundered after six of the proposed twenty-four volumes had been published. Dom Martin Bouquet was put in charge, and the work, entitled *Rerum gallicarum et francicarum scriptores*, but usually known by the first word of its French title as Bouquet's *Recueil*, ran to thirteen volumes between 1737 and 1786. It is in a sense the grandmother of all the great national collections: of the *Monumenta*, the Rolls Series, the Swedish, Danish and Portuguese *Rerum scriptores*.

Yet another heavy vessel was getting under way at the same time, the *Histoire littéraire de la France*, which, begun as a solo performance by Dom Rivet, by the outbreak of the Revolution had reached its twelfth volume and the middle of the twelfth century. But indeed there is no end to the Maurist catalogue, even if works of history alone are admitted, for besides a proposed edition of the councils of the French church, of the letters of the popes and of the historians of the crusades, a great series of monographs on the provinces and cities of the country poured forth during the eighteenth century, many of them containing the finest and most careful work of the scattered workers of the second rank in abbeys and priories throughout France.

Finally, a word should be said of the part taken by the Maurists in developing what are called the auxiliary sciences of history. Their most outstanding contribution has already been mentioned: the virtual creation of the sciences of medieval and Byzantine palaeography by Mabillon and Montfaucon. Of the two, Mabillon contributed far more than Montfaucon, for besides the strictly diplomatic and palaeographical parts of his great treatise, he helped on their way a whole group of lesser partners, such as numismatics and sphragistics. Only less important than the work of these two scholars was that of the group who produced the great treatise which they called *L'Art de vérifier les dates*. Like all similar works which include detailed lists and computations—like our own *Handbook of British Chronology*—it has proved peculiarly susceptible of correction and improvement, and has long been superseded, but for almost a century it was a vade-mecum of historians, and modern treatises and handbooks all trace a part at least of their ancestry to it.

Besides these major works, the Maurists were the first to provide themselves with a series of bibliographical 'aids.' The first two were due to the enterprise of Dom Tarrisse and Dom d'Achery; they were a list of books that all libraries of the congregation should aim at possessing, and a directive, compiled by d'Achery at the request of Dom Tarrisse, to all houses as to the methods of research and the objects to be pursued in compiling the domestic history of the place. Mabillon, for his part, was responsible for two 'guides'; the one, a revised and enlarged version of d'Achery's circular, was his *Avis pour ceux qui travaillent aux histoires des monastères* (1677); the other was the long 'reading-list' that formed part of his *Traité des études*. To these must be added the great catalogue of manuscripts, already mentioned, compiled by Montfaucon, and the revision of Du Cange's *Glossarium* in 1733-6. It may indeed be said that the Maurists were the first body of historical scholars to realize not only the advantages and possibilities but also the needs of large-scale group-work, and therefore the first to provide tools and instructions, and to plan with an eye on the distant future. In this respect, at least, all subsequent institutes, academies and publishing committees of historians have derived, at first or last remove, guidance and inspiration from their achievement.[1]

The Maurists, like the Bollandists, were among

---

[1] C. V. Langlois, *Manuel [de bibliographie historique]* (2 vols., Paris 1904), II, pp. 296-7, remarks: 'On a pu, depuis, perfectionner ces ouvrages; mais les grandes lignes n'en ont pas bougé: les disciplines auxiliaires du moyen âge ont gardé jusqu'à nos jours la physionomie que les Mauristes leur ont donnée.'

the many casualties of the Revolution. Unlike the Bollandists, they did not again come into being when peace returned to Europe. The Congregation of France, that owed its form to Dom Guéranger, respected the Maurist past, and many of its sons have taken inspiration from Saint-Germain, but it was in every way a new creation, with a traditional and different organization.

Nevertheless, what we may call 'Maurism' had a notable posthumous career. The literary remains of the monks scattered throughout the municipal and departmental archives of France survive principally in the Bibliothèque Nationale, where they have provided, and still provide, almost inexhaustible mineral wealth for historians and antiquaries, all the more so since transcripts and plans made by the Maurists are often the only witness that remains of charters and vanished abbeys. Next, there were the editions of the Fathers and medieval writers. Many of these continued to provide a steady income for publishers throughout the nineteenth century, and there must be few medievalists with European interests who have not one or more volumes on their shelves. They also proved a godsend to the Abbé Migne. Guéranger and Pitra, who acted as his advisers in early days, made full use of the Maurists, and the *Patrologiae* would have been far less valuable had their texts been unavailable; Migne also took the notes and prefaces of d'Achery, Mabillon and the rest, and reprinted them unchanged, save for a liberal scattering of misprints.

Over and above this, four at least of the great

enterprises were resumed by other hands in the new age. The first, and least notable, was the continuation, in 1870, of the *Monasticum Gallicanum*[1] after a lapse of almost exactly two centuries. The *Gallia Christiana*, which was within sight of land at the Revolution, was completed *tant bien que mal* by B. Hauréau with the addition of three volumes covering Tours, Besançon (Vesontio) and Vienne (1856, 1860, 1865). As in the parallel case of the *Monasticon Anglicanum*, the volumes remain an indispensable but wholly inadequate work of reference, which all scholars would wish to see replaced, though the bravest heart would quail at the prospect of undertaking the task.[2] Two other works had somewhat better fortune. Bouquet's *Recueil*[3] was still in active course of production at the Revolution, and one of the collaborators, Dom Brial, retained many of the materials and continued, as *citoyen* Brial, to function as a man of letters in Paris throughout the years of upheaval. In the early years of the Empire the *Institut de France*, which replaced the suppressed academies of the old regime,[4] undertook the continuation of the work, which was soon deputed to the *Académie des Inscriptions et Belles-Lettres*, of

[1] For this, see *D.A.C*, xi, pp. 2190–2204.

[2] Brief notes on the *Gallia Christiana* are in Langlois, *Manuel*, i, pp. 297–8, and L. Halphen, *Initiation [aux études d'histoire du moyen âge]* (Paris 1946), pp. 102–3. cf. also Pécheur, 'Précis sur l'histoire du Gallia Christiana,' in *Bulletin de la Société archéologique de Soissons*, xv (1884), p. 127.

[3] For the Recueil, see Langlois, *Manuel*, ii, pp. 298–9, 374–5, and Halphen, *Initiation*, pp. 67–8.

[4] There is a short account of the re-creation of the various Instituts and Académies, 1795–1832, in Langlois, *Manuel*, ii, pp. 371–2.

which Dom Brial was elected a member. He was responsible, between 1806 and 1822, for five volumes, and the *Académie des Inscriptions* continued to be in charge throughout the nineteenth century; six more volumes appeared, the twenty-fourth and last in 1904. Gradually, however, the character of the enterprise changed. From being a collection (like our Rolls Series) of Annals and Chronicles it came to include record and economic material of all kinds. Indeed, it gradually became so amorphous and endless that sixty years ago it was decided to discontinue the work altogether. Meanwhile, a reimpression of the earlier volumes had been put in hand (from 1869), with the (at first glance) curious result that an early volume of a complete set may bear a later date than one that comes after it in the original series.

A somewhat similar, though on the whole more kindly, fate overtook the *Histoire littéraire* of Dom Rivet.[1] Here the last Benedictine volume had appeared in 1763, when the twelfth century had been reached. A committee of the reconstituted *Institut* took up the enterprise in 1807 with Dom Brial as one of the small commission, and vols. XIII–XVI were produced, after the fashion of the pre-Revolution volumes, before his death. He was succeeded as editor by the ex-Oratorian Père C. F. Daunon (d. 1840) and a gradual change began. Vernacular literature, which had formed no part of the original work, was dealt with and greater attention was paid to the individual

---

[1] Langlois, *Manuel*, II, pp. 299–300, 375–6; Halphen, *Initiation*, pp. 126–7. There is an interesting account of the development of the work by Langlois in the introduction to vol. XXXVI (1927).

writer and his works. From 1865 onwards the change was still more pronounced. A small commission of eminent scholars versed in history, literature and the new skills of philology produced a series of brilliant monographs with little or no connection with each other; names such as Emile Littré, Ernest Renan, Barthélemy Hauréau, Léopold Delisle, Gaston Paris, C. V. Langlois, Paul Fournier and their peers are a sufficient guarantee of the value and high scholarship of the work, but the series has become steadily more and more monographic in character, with many studies dealing with a single class of literature such as vernacular chansons or canon-law studies. Moreover, there has been an increasing tendency to stray into by-ways, and to return in circles to pick up lost companions and signalize new discoveries. As a result, during the last hundred years, the work has advanced chronologically by only half a century, and there would seem to be every likelihood that the Bollandists will have no difficulty in beating the *Institut* to the tape. As for the Maurists, one feels they would have had the thing done in a workmanlike way fifty years ago.

The work of the Maurists remains, and may well remain for centuries to come, the most impressive achievement of co-operative, or at least co-ordinated, scholarship in the modern world. Alike in the boldness and the wisdom of its planning, the skill and success of its organization, the industry and long perseverance of its execution, and the high technical and intellectual quality of its content, the body of the Maurist work is a unique phenomenon in the history of scholarship. In mere bulk the printed output overwhelms the imagination of the beholder, and when we remember that for many of the Fathers and medieval writers the Maurist text and edition is still the most convenient, and sometimes also the best, available, our admiration comes to equal our amazement. Perhaps no-one will appreciate this more fully than one who has himself lived and known the monastic life in more than one of its present-day manifestations, and who has had experience of the variety of talent and temperament, enthusiasm and discouragement, occupations and hopes, that every monastic family harbours in its midst.

That there should have been found, for well over a century, a constant supply of men equipped in mind and character with the qualifications fitting them to take a useful part in such a mass production of learned work is not the least of the glories of the French genius. Indeed, the Maurists, or the minority of scholars among the Maurists, have succeeded in imposing upon the mind of educated Europe that they were the monastic norm, and not the brilliant exceptions, and that all other Benedictines were as they. Through their achievement the adjective 'learned' has come to be attached, as an *epitheton constans*, to the name of Benedictine, and no higher praise can be given to a monastic scholar than to call him a Maurist of today.

The *Monumenta Germaniae Historica*

The only adequate account in English of German historical studies in the nineteenth century is the old, but still valuable, *History and Historians in the nineteenth century*, by G. P. Gooch (London 1913; 3rd ed. revised 1952); there is a section on the *Monumenta*, and a short account of Waitz.

For the story of the *M[onumenta] G[ermaniae] H[istorica]* to 1921 the narrative by Harry Bresslau, the official centenary historian, in *N[eues] A[rchiv]*, XLII (1921), is authoritative, and has been followed throughout. References are given as *Bresslau*. It may be supplemented by Wattenbach-Levison-Holtzmann, *Deutschlands Geschichtsquellen in Mittelalter* (ed. 1952), II, pp. 17–28; G. Waitz, 'Über die Zukunft der M.G.H.,' in *Historische Zeitschrift*, XXX (1873), pp. 1–13; and E. Dümmler, 'Über die Entstehung der M.G.H.,' in *Im neuen Reich* (Leipzig 1876). A volume by H. Heimpel, *Organisationsformen deutscher Geschichtswissenschaft*, commemorating the centenary of the birth of P. F. Kehr, was scheduled for publication early in 1960 (Göttingen-Zürich).

3

The *Monumenta Germaniae Historica*

LAST December we considered the work of the
Maurists, who were at once a product and an
ornament of a very brilliant phase of French learning
and scholarship. This afternoon we turn to another
great nation in what was, perhaps, the golden age of
its influence upon the thought and academic disciplines of Europe.

German scholarship of the nineteenth century,
and in particular German historical scholarship, was
for long unduly neglected in this country. Then, for
a short space between the wars of 1870 and 1914,
it was widely admired and imitated. Finally, as a
result of the two wars and the Nazi regime, it has
in large part fallen once more out of the picture for
Englishmen, and its achievements and the names of
its most eminent practitioners have all but passed
into oblivion. It may therefore be of interest to rescue
from this undeserved neglect a great enterprise
which, initiated by a single man, grew to be a focus
of technical scholarship unequalled even in Germany,
and ended by becoming a national, not to say a
nationalized or Nazialized, institution.

The 'only begetter' of the *Monumenta* was the
eminent Prussian statesman and patriot, the Baron
Karl von Stein. Stein was a statesman of energy,

foresight, honesty and determination whose greatness, on a long view, must be reckoned indisputable.[1]
He was also a man of wide intelligence and culture,
with a particular interest in history, and a conviction
that nothing would better serve the cause of German
nationhood than a full knowledge of the medieval
Empire. Retiring into private life after the Congress
of Vienna, he had leisure to use his influence and
means in furthering his ideas. He had discussed his
hopes with friends such as the brothers Grimm,
Goethe, Eichhorn and Savigny, and a number of
proposals had been made, among others one of
Wessenberg for a network of central and regional
associations with government funds and princely
patronage. This and other schemes like it broke
down upon the hard reef of finance, and the actual
beginning was due to Stein alone who enlisted the
help of two scholars, Büchler and Dümgé, the latter
of whom drew up a prospectus of a publishing and
editing society (24 June 1818), while Stein began a
search for subscribers. Finally, a meeting took place
at Frankfurt on 20 January 1819, at which Stein and
four leading politicians agreed on a plan establishing
Dümgé as general editor and Büchler as secretary of
the enterprise, and on 12 June the constitutions of a
society, *Die Gesellschaft für Deutschlands ältere*

---

[1] Stein's biography has been written by G. H. Pertz (6 vols. in 7,
1849–55), Sir J. M. Seeley, *The Life and Times of Stein* (3 vols., 1878),
and G. Ritter, *Stein, eine politische Biographie*, 2 vols. (Stuttgart-Berlin
1931; repr. 1958). For a short account, see the article by J. Holland Rose
in *Encyclopaedia Britannica*, 11th ed. (1911). Stein was assisted by
others, especially by J. A. v. Aretin, but the latter is not entitled to the
share attributed to him in *N.D.B.*, s.v. Aretin, J. A.

Geschichtskunde, were approved, and remained in force (if that is the word) for more than fifty years.

The association thus called into being had an unusual organization. Whereas a society is normally directed by officers elected from among its members, here from the first the members were contradistinguished from the directorate or governing body (*Direktion* or *Zentraldirektion*) under a president. No machinery was set up for the appointment of editor and secretary, who were not *ex officio* members of the directorate. Stein was, as if by nature, president, and it was assumed that he would appoint the two officers. Members, who became so at first by invitation of Stein or the directorate, had no right or voice in the affairs of the society; their numbers never increased, and in fact diminished in time almost to vanishing-point. In other words, the society was one of straw; all duties and power lay with the president and the two officers.

Neither Dümgé, a sour and difficult man, nor Büchler, who lacked technical competence, was capable of getting the undertaking out of harbour and over the bar, and by the end of 1821 the former had been dropped by Stein while the latter, who had tried to defend his friend, had resigned. Meanwhile Stein had displayed the greatest energy in finding friends and funds, and among his minor achievements may be counted his enlistment of Goethe, whom he set collating a manuscript of Otto of Freising. Nevertheless, the going was not good; Stein himself had to find most of the money to support the first researches, and a considerable sum was lost on useless or senseless travel in search of manuscripts on the part of inefficient collaborators. The situation was saved by the fortunate appearance of Georg Heinrich Pertz (1795–1876).

Pertz[1] came from Hanover, the son and grandson of prosperous bookbinders; as a schoolboy he had seen and experienced the rigours of the French occupation. Educated in classics and history at Göttingen, he was engaged as tutor in Hanover to a family with official and diplomatic connections which made him familiar with the tastes and manners of high society and ultimately brought him into personal and friendly contact with Stein. Pertz as a young man was highly intelligent, vivacious, good looking and in every way presentable, and in his early life, at least, lacked neither charm nor understanding nor sympathy. He was sent by Stein to search out manuscripts at Vienna, and his work, and still more his success in personal relations, led Stein to send him in the autumn of 1821 to Rome. Here his tact and charm made still further conquests; he made the acquaintance of Consalvi and Mai and, contrary to all expectation, received the entrée to the Vatican archives. He also won the confidence and affection of the great Niebuhr, then acting as Prussian representative to the Vatican, and was treated by him as a family friend, almost as a son. When, therefore, Stein was faced with the crisis of 1821 and had tried

[1] There is no adequate life of Pertz. An interesting autobiographical fragment, dictated to his second wife in 1869, together with a selection of his letters (in English), was published by Leonora Pertz in ?1894. His letters to Droysen were published in 1896. Bresslau was able to use many others in the archives of *M.G.H.* For Pertz see also *A.D.B.*

more than one shift, he finally turned to his brilliant young protégé and on 26 August 1823 it was settled that Pertz should become the society's editor. It was a piece of extraordinary good fortune for the undertaking. Pertz, forty years later, was to suffer an eclipse, and to arouse criticism, opposition, and even hostility, but by then much water had flowed under the bridges, and in 1823 Stein could scarcely have found a better man in Germany to combine the enterprise of youth with solid scholarship and an admirable capacity both for organization and for hard work, together with the determination that could carry him through weather both fair and foul.

Meanwhile Stein had also found his secretary. Johann Friedrich Böhmer[1] was a young man of exactly the same age as Pertz (1795–1863) but of a very different character and temperament. He was a Frankfurter of the upper bourgeoisie, whose father had held high civic office with conservative traditions from the pre-Napoleonic age; he was earnest, thrifty, retiring and far from expansive in society, but he was loyal, sensitive and romantic of mind. Throughout his life he felt a deep attraction towards the traditions and external manifestations of the Catholic Church, and he had many friends and disciples of that faith, such as Brentano and Janssen, but he never took the step of joining the Church. His influence over a school of historians was considerable, but lies outside our scope. Stein, who had known his family in

---

[1] For Böhmer, see the biography, *J. F. Böhmer's Leben, Briefe, etc.*, by J. Janssen (1868). cf. also Ranke, *Abhandlungen und Versuche*, Neue Sammlung, pp. 535–44.

other years, met him and offered him the post of
secretary. In August 1823 Böhmer met Pertz, and
wrote of him as a future Mabillon of Germany; Pertz
for his part took to Böhmer and the long association,
which ripened into a friendship, began that was to
survive all trials and differences until it was broken
by death.

Now that Stein had two such excellent officers it
was possible to devise a programme. From the beginning the conception was grandiose: all the sources
(Stein would rather have said, all the memorials) of
German history from the disappearance of effective
Roman rule to the invention of printing—in other
words, the millennium from A.D. 500 to 1500. The
only topics excluded, large indeed in themselves, but
necessarily left on one side, were the purely ecclesiastical history of Germany, and the crusades. The
materials were from the first divided into five sections,
namely chronicles (*Scriptores*), laws (*Leges*), charters
(*Diplomata*), letters (*Epistolae*), and finally writings of
antiquarian interest (*Antiquitates*). Hahn of Hanover
was selected as publisher.

The first task of the new editor was to produce a
volume which would attract attention and prove the
viability of Stein's enterprise. Logically, a beginning
should have been made with the early Merovingian
documents, but this was a peculiarly difficult field in
which Pertz had as yet no materials. It was decided
therefore to begin with Charlemagne, and the first
volume duly appeared on 14 August 1826 with the
subtitle *Annales et Chronica aevi Carolini*. After
some discussion the format of royal folio had been

selected, and from the various formulae proposed by Pertz for the general name of the series Stein selected the familiar three words: MONUMENTA GERMANIAE HISTORICA. On the title-page was the motto originally suggested by Büchler, which has become familiar to so many thousands of readers: 'Sanctus amor patriae dat animum.'

No sooner had the first volume appeared than Pertz set out in search of manuscripts to Paris and England. His reputation, his charm and his ability to combine hard work with social activities were remarkable; in Paris he was received not only by Rémusat, Guérard and the Thierrys, but in diplomatic circles and in fashionable salons. He found manuscripts in plenty; he also found a wife in Julia Garnett, the American-born daughter of a well-known English astronomer. They were married in Paris, with Lafayette and the Hanoverian minister among the guests, and returned to Hanover after Pertz had taken his wife to stay with Niebuhr and Stein, who found her intelligent, unaffected and winning. In the autumn of this year (1827) Pertz entered upon his duties at Hanover as archivist and librarian of the Royal Library.

In December 1829 the second volume appeared, largely the work of Pertz. Taken together, the first two volumes, with a total of 1,500 folio pages, were a good beginning. Several important works, such as the *Annales Xantenses*, discovered by Pertz, were published for the first time, others, such as Einhard's Life of Charlemagne, appeared in a vastly improved text, and though here and there later critics could find faults, the favourable reception was justified. Difficulties, however, were by no means over. Energetic as he was, Pertz could not alone do all the editorial and sub-editorial work, and in 1829 he secured his first standing collaborator, a man of his own age, J. M. Lappenberg, state archivist of Hamburg. Lappenberg did excellent work and remained a pillar of the *Monumenta* till his death forty years later, but he was a contributor, not an assistant. The same may be said of the somewhat unexpected emergence of Böhmer. Böhmer had long been anxious to help with the scholarship as well as with the administration, and had already collected materials for small undertakings. Now, inspired by Pertz, he volunteered to compile a register of imperial charters from 911 to 1313 to serve as the first volume of the *Diplomata* section. The first part was out in 1831 and the series, with offshoots and revisions, continued till his death, but it was financed by Böhmer himself and did not figure among the *Monumenta*, though it usually finds a place on the shelves alongside. With all its inevitable faults and errors it was not only a priceless tool but an inspiration and a pioneer in an important field.

Meanwhile the financial position was still stringent. Neither governments nor nobles helped as Stein had hoped. Some feared, as in France in the days of the Maurists, that research might upset the titles of the reigning houses and powerful families; others, that a study of medieval Germany would make men anti-liberal and pro-Catholic.[1] Metternich in parti-

[1] For this, see Waitz, *N.A.*, II, p. 460.

cular feared revolutionary discoveries and would not allow Austria to help. Before any firm position had been reached the undertaking lost its only powerful guide and support with the unexpected death of Stein (29 June 1831). This event revealed the faulty organization of the society. Neither Pertz nor Böhmer was a member of the directorate; the only efficient member to hand was the Prussian politician and minister, Baron K. F. F. von Nagler. Fortunately, the financial cares of the *Monumenta* were shortly to be eased. Böhmer was tireless in circularizing ministers and politicians, and Nagler used his influence in high quarters. Now that Stein was dead Metternich was no longer hostile, and at the Vienna conference of 1834 he recommended the appeal to the Federal Assembly; this body in turn recommended a block grant to be raised by contributions from the member states. The total sum was paltry, and the inevitable shuffling and haggling took place while everyone waited for his neighbour to move, but eventually an income was assured,[1] for a few years only but renewable, and with no strings attached save a very reasonable demand for yearly accounts and report of progress. A more favourable arrangement was made in 1844. Having achieved this, Nagler withdrew into the shadows, leaving Pertz and Böhmer in power. In Stein's project the directorate was to be composed of statesmen and dignitaries, employing an editor and secretary. The constitution remained in force but the president had

---

[1] *Bresslau*, p. 209, gives it as nearly 5,000 Taler per annum. The monetary reckonings of early days are always in Gulden and Taler.

vanished, leaving editor and secretary as sole directors. For thirty years the *Monumenta* was to be conducted by two men living far apart, drawing annual funds from the Federal Assembly, and in fact responsible to no-one. Pertz was by far the more powerful of the two partners, but Böhmer was a faithful and active manager, who did not fail to make his views known, though in the final resort Pertz usually had his way.

Shortly after the financial settlement Pertz secured his first regular assistants. The great resurgence of historical activity had by now begun to pay dividends. Above all, Ranke at Berlin had founded a school that was to influence all Europe.[1] Besides his fame as a writer and a personality, which only Macaulay among living historians could rival, Ranke was one of the greatest of academic teachers. He did not indeed initiate, but he certainly canonized, the *Seminar*, a group of promising pupils to whom the master taught the skills of his craft in co-operative work with mutual help and rivalry in the field of his own studies. Ranke also gave his pupils two revolutionary methods—recourse to records and archives, rather than to literary sources, and the thorough criticism of the reliability and characteristics of all the contemporary witnesses. His fame attracted students from the whole of central Europe and beyond and for half a century the cream of German scholarship flowed through his hands.

Ranke initiated his seminar in 1833, and in the group of the first two years were Giesebrecht, Köpke,

---

[1] For a short English account of Ranke, see Gooch, op. cit., chap. vi.

Hirsch and Waitz. The last-named,[1] who had come to Ranke by way of Savigny and Lachmann, was hailed by the master as the future Muratori of Germany; in 1835 he won a prize for a brilliant study of King Henry I, and at the advice of Lappenberg, warmly recommended by Ranke, he offered his services to Pertz, who thus in 1836 acquired without effort and for a subsistence wage the greatest medieval scholar of the century, who as a critic was to revolutionize the study of sources and as a constitutional historian did for Germany what Stubbs, his admirer, was later to do for England. In 1837 Waitz was joined by another able young man, Ludwig Bethmann. Both lived with Pertz and his alert, sympathetic and kindly wife as members of the family; the Pertz of those days was still the lovable master and friend; Waitz describes him in his diary as a frank, homely man, with blond hair, blue eyes and an open forehead, a leader, but approachable. It was the April of the *Monumenta*.

The *Scriptores* continued to appear at regular intervals, and as early as 1829 there began a series of individual texts reprinted with shorter editorial matter in cheaper octavo form *in usum scholarum*. At a later date, the 'school' editions became new, scholarly editions replacing many of the original

---

[1] There is no good biography of Waitz; for an intimate sketch by his son Eberhard, see *Georg Waitz* (Berlin 1913; the centenary of his birth). For appreciations, see W. Wattenbach, *Abhandlungen d. Berliner Akademie* (1886); A. Kluckhohn, 'Zur Erinnerung an Georg Waitz,' in *Sammlung Gemeinverständlicher wissenschaftlicher Vorträge* (ed. Virchov u. Holtzendorff), N.F., ii Ser., Heft. 25–48 (Berlin 1887), pp. 347–82, and the attractive pages of G. Monod in *Portraits et Souvenirs* (1897).

folios. From these arose a controversy between
Pertz and Böhmer which lasted for more than
thirty years. Pertz throughout loved the folio format, and viewed with displeasure both the proposal
to reduce the *Scriptores* to quarto or to publish
a simultaneous octavo version. He feared loss of
sales and diversion of editorial energy. Böhmer,
with more prophetic vision, wished to popularize
scholarly and historical work as much as possible.
Unable to move Pertz, he himself produced, outside the *Monumenta*, a series of small volumes of
texts with introductory matter, each grouped round
a leading topic, under the title *Fontes Rerum Germanicarum*. The first appeared in 1843, and the series
had a wide sale.

While the financial position was still stringent, a
great change had taken place in Pertz's life. In 1841
Ranke, supported by Jacob Grimm and Savigny,
obtained for him the offer of the Directorate of the
Royal Library in Berlin. Pertz, after some hard
bargaining, accepted the post and in April 1842
moved into the commodious house adjoining the
great library; he was soon joined by Waitz. A new
chapter opened for the *Monumenta*; Pertz, with the
entrée to official and academic circles, the friend of
Bekker, of Lachmann, of the Grimms, of Schelling
and of Meineke, was now a state official, and in
two years' time the new grant enabled him to
establish for the first time a rudimentary staff. It
is true that in 1842 he lost the direct services of
Waitz, who went to a chair at Kiel and later (1849)
at Göttingen, where he founded a seminar in

medieval history that was to become celebrated, but Waitz ever remained faithful to the *Monumenta* and his old chief. Meanwhile, Pertz had found two excellent successors, Rudolf Köpke, Waitz's companion of old under Ranke, and Wilhelm Wattenbach,[1] a pupil of Otfried Müller who, initiated by Ranke, Hirsch and Giesebrecht, came to the *Monumenta* in 1843. These with Waitz and Bethmann were the first professional 'Monumentists,' 'Pertz's boys' as Edmund Bishop used to call them, and the chief could now work to a programme with a regular conference on Saturday evenings, though then as always he left great freedom of choice in subject and method to his assistants. It was now, probably through the initiative of Waitz, that a typographical innovation of importance occurred. It had been customary for some years to note in the margin the source, if known, of the medieval writer's text; now the practice was begun of printing all that could be traced to an earlier source in small type, thus making clear at a glance not only the general but even the verbal dependence of a chronicler upon his predecessors.

The years that followed saw the arrival and departure of several talented men. The volumes of *Scriptores* continued to appear, and the name occurred for the first time of Philipp Jaffé, in some ways the most brilliant of all 'Pertz's boys.' Jaffé, a young Jew, had abandoned the commercial career planned for him, and spent some months

[1] For Wattenbach, see Dümmler's Gedächtnisrede in *Abhandlungen d. Berliner Akademie* (1892).

with Ranke. Pertz, despite unfavourable criticism,
became his patron, and Jaffé, in five years of phenomenal activity, produced the first (1851) edition of
his well-known Register of papal letters. Pertz continued his help, and endeavoured to obtain for him
access to the papal archives for a continuation of his
work. Pio Nono, however, though courteous, was
not forthcoming, and Jaffé in 1854 accepted an
invitation to join the staff of the *Monumenta* where,
for the next dozen years, he was responsible for
much of the best work. Pertz showed less judgment
in the encouragement he gave to his eldest son Karl,
whom in the same year he made a permanent assistant. Karl was a good worker but without a touch of
brilliance; he lacked perception and technical skill,
while remaining extremely self-satisfied. Differing
in every way as they did, these two recruits
were destined to be the principal causes of Pertz's
undoing.

Meanwhile Pertz's private life had undergone
another change. His first wife had died in 1852.
In 1854 he married another Englishwoman, Leonora
Horner, a daughter of the well-known geologist and
educationist, Leonard Horner,[1] for long a chief
inspector under the Factories Act. Miss Horner's
sisters had married respectively Sir Charles Lyell,[2]
the eminent geologist, and Sir Charles Bunbury,[3] a
baronet of ancient family with property at Mildenhall
and Barton, near Cambridge. These connections
brought Pertz into touch with people of rank and

[1] See *D.N.B.*, s.v.   [2] ibid.
[3] ibid., for article on his father.

influence in England, and undoubtedly helped him in his researches; he was admitted to the libraries of Earl Spencer and Lord Ashburnham as a gentleman as well as a scholar; we find him staying at Battle and at Barton Hall, and still more unexpectedly joining holiday groups at Tenby and Barmouth, while in Berlin he was seen at government receptions, ambassadorial soirées, and dinners of the English colony. Nevertheless, the influence of his second wife was not wholly benign; she was less adaptable and less motherly; she returned to England for her confinements to give her children English nationality, and insisted on English ways in her house; English was the language of general use there. The young Monumentists were no longer a part of the family, and this circumstance, added to others, made Pertz less approachable. For a time, however, all went well. Merkel and Bluhme produced a valuable volume of *Laws* (the third) in 1863, and two more recruits of worth appeared in Winkelmann,[1] the first of Waitz's pupils, and Arndt,[2] pupil of Ranke and Waitz. Against the excellent work of these and others had to be set some less successful editing of Pertz himself. Pertz was hardening in every way, and his aloofness towards his juniors may have hastened, though it certainly did not cause, the tragic dénouement of his relations with Jaffé. It would appear that Pertz in 1860 was responsible for blocking an offer made to Jaffé of an important post in the Florence archives.

[1] 1838–96. For him and the other scholars of the *M.G.H.*, the Nachruf or short obituary in the *N.A.* may be consulted; here the reference is *N.A.*, XXI, pp. 770ff.; see also *A.D.B.*

[2] 1838–95. *N.A.*, XX, pp. 664ff.; *A.D.B.* (supplement).

The matter rankled, and in 1862 Jaffé unexpectedly served on Pertz (who happened to be in Glasgow) the requisite six months' notice of withdrawal from the *Monumenta*. Pertz, stung by what he considered the ingratitude of his ablest lieutenant, accepted the notice but held Jaffé to his six months. Jaffé was still more embittered; he had friends in Berlin such as Ranke, Haupt, Mommsen, Dümmler and Wattenbach, all of whom took his part against Pertz. It was the beginning of a sad ten years in the life of the *Monumenta* and its chief. In the autumn of 1863, Pertz lost his loyal partner Böhmer, with whom he had often disagreed but never quarrelled, and who had often given good counsel. He was now monarch of the *Monumenta* and at sixty-eight showed no sign of choosing a partner or successor. Both the scholars who bought his goods and the politicians who supplied the funds felt that some control or at least a wider spread of responsibility was needed. Relations were embittered by the secretive habits of Pertz, who refused to allow scholars, even such a one as Sickel, to use materials accumulated twenty or thirty years earlier for future use.

The head and front of Pertz's offending, however, was his treatment of the *Monumenta* as private property, to be inherited by his son Karl, while he based his position on the constitution of a virtually extinct society. For months the intrigues continued. Bismarck was approached and endeavoured to withdraw the affair from the Federal Assembly to his own jurisdiction. Pertz fought back with the utmost pertinacity and adroitness. Twice when all seemed lost he was

saved first by Bismarck's distraction in the Schleswig-
Holstein crisis and later by the dissolution of the
Confederacy on the outbreak of war with Austria,
as a result of which Prussia assumed liability for the
finances of the *Monumenta*. But though he had
undoubtedly won the first round, the skies continued to darken. Waitz remained faithful and with
his old genius for selection Pertz acquired Weiland,[1]
a pupil of Waitz, in 1865 and Scheffer-Boichorst,[2]
pupil of Waitz and Köpke, in 1871; these two became
firm friends and did yeoman service in after years.
On the other hand, the final breach had come with
Jaffé. On leaving the *Monumenta* he had planned a
series of historical texts, mainly letters, centering
round personalities and places, critically edited and
annotated; the project had the blessing of Mommsen,
and the first volumes had a great success. The series
was taken by Pertz, and probably intended by Jaffé,
to be a competitor of the cheap editions in the
Monumenta; he retorted by every kind of petty foot-
note insult, while Jaffé heaped fuel on the fire by
publishing an edition of the letters of St Boniface,
long projected and promised by Pertz, and by sharp
criticism of Pertz's scholarship. Finally, Jaffé had
the misfortune to lose a manuscript from the Berlin
library, whereupon Pertz forbade him the use of the
place, and when the Minister stepped in on Jaffé's
behalf proceeded to accuse his old assistant of
espionage. The matter now passed to the lawyers;
Pertz refused to withdraw the charge and Jaffé

[1] 1841–95.
[2] 1843–1902. *N.A.*, xxvii, pp. 768ff.; *A.D.B.*

circulated widely in official and academic circles a burning rebuttal. His mind had long had a streak of morbidity, and he now developed a mania of hatred and persecution; in 1870, at the height of his powers as a scholar, he took his own life. For this Pertz cannot be held accountable,[1] but he himself was now showing signs of age and even of an unbalanced mind.[2] Hopeless anarchy reigned in the management of the *Monumenta*; editions languished and proofs were not sent to the editors. Even Waitz determined to contribute no more; Köpke was removed by death, and the first volume of the *Diplomata*, edited by Karl Pertz, was a thoroughly unsatisfactory piece of work. These and similar misfortunes led the government, spurred on by Ranke, to act, and a commission was set up to report. For six months the affair dragged on. Pertz, by a mixture of masterly inaction and historical and legal special pleading, defeated all efforts and resisted all appeals; it was his duty as Stein's legatee to hold on to the *Monumenta*. Finally, in February 1873, when his opponents, *de guerre lasse*, had decided that they must wait for him to die, Pertz suddenly and unconditionally threw in his hand. He was treated with great respect and allowed to share in the rearrangement, but in fact took no further share in the business. He had previously been forced to leave the library,

---

[1] The article on Jaffé in *A.D.B.*, by Alfred Dove, is unjustifiably harsh in its tone towards Pertz.

[2] *Bresslau*, citing Wattenbach, p. 469. cf. Dümmler to Sickel, 28 August 1872: 'Pertz ist geistig stumpf, hält aber gleichwohl mit unbeugsamer Energie den Besitz der Monumenta als Familieneigentum fest' (*Bresslau*, p. 469, n. 1).

and his last few years were spent in darkening shadows though his wife and family were loyal.

The interested scholars now became active. Waitz, who had refused to move against his old master, was now persuaded to act, and the *Monumenta* was entrusted to a new directorate. This was to include two members nominated by the three academies of Berlin, Munich and Vienna; the rest were to be chosen by co-optation, and were to elect a president, who was himself to have charge of the *Scriptores*.[1] The new directorate was a strong one; Mommsen, Sickel, Giesebrecht, Wattenbach, Dümmler were among its members, with Pertz and Euler carried over from the past. Von Sybel was among the early additions. The directorate was to meet yearly to settle matters of high policy; a committee, consisting of those resident in Berlin, dealt with business in the interim. To each of the five sections leaders were to be appointed with an *ex-officio* seat on the directorate. Ample government funds were granted for the work in general and specifically for a salary for Waitz, together with official quarters and a room for the *Monumenta*. In the autumn of 1875 Waitz left Göttingen to take up his duties. Pertz, greatly decayed in his powers, was present at the annual general meeting in 1876; he died of a stroke in the autumn. A final judgment on his scholarship and on his character has yet to be made, and it may well be more favourable than that of the historian whose account we have been following; here alone perhaps does he seem to lose

[1] For the new statutes, see *N.A.*, i, pp. 7–9.

his fine impartiality. In any case, Pertz had done an inestimable service to European scholarship. To him in another, but in as real a way as to Stein, the *Monumenta* owed its existence. Ranke, who was not always among his supporters, may be allowed the last word. 'In the end,' he wrote, 'we are told, he became dull and apathetic. That cannot prevent me from recognizing the great significance of his life. He was not a genius, but he was of sterling worth.' [1]

The new directorate got speedily down to work, and the *Monumenta* entered upon the golden age of its existence. Waitz himself took the *Scriptores*, always recognized as the core of the enterprise, but the early, half-Roman period was shorn off as a province for Mommsen. For the *Laws*, always the *Schmerzenskind* of the family,[2] Boretius of Halle, an old Monumentist who had fallen foul of Pertz, was proposed, but both Waitz and Mommsen vetoed him, and Waitz kept the section in hand. Sickel, the eminent Vienna palaeographer,[3] took the *Diplomata*, which henceforth were domesticated in Austria; Wattenbach, unwillingly, took the *Letters*; Dümmler at his own wish the *Antiquities*. The funds available were stepped up in 1876 and again in 1880. Other

[1] Ranke, *Ges. Werke*, LIV, pp. 610 ff.: 'Er war nicht genial, aber gediegen.' Perhaps 'solid' is a better translatian of 'gediegen'.

[2] The phrase is used of a later period by Paul Kehr in his memoir of E. Seckel, *N.A.*, XLVI, p. 160: 'Die Leges sind von Anfang an das grosse Schmerzenskind der Monumenta gewesen.'

[3] Theodor v. Sickel, 1826–1908. For him, see *Bresslau*, p. 400, note, Erben in *Historische Vierteljahrschrift*, XI, pp. 333ff., L. Santifaller (editor), *Theodor v. Sickel, Römische Erinnerungen* (Vienna 1947), and W. Holtzmann in *Archivio della società Romana di storia patria*, LXXIX (1956), pp. 89ff.

significant changes were made; the folio format was abandoned for all sections save the *Scriptores* in favour of the quarto. There was a discussion on the use of Latin for editorial matter; in the end it was retained for all save the vernacular texts, but Latin was not Sickel's strong suit, and after he had, with assistance, produced one introduction the learned tongue was abandoned in the *Diplomata*.[1] The octavo series of *Scriptores rerum Germanicarum* was developed. Perhaps the greatest surprise was the emergence of Mommsen, already in his mid-sixties, as the energetic and prolific editor who speedily made his section the most brilliant of all. Doubts were expressed then and later as to the relevance of some of the late classical authors, such as Symmachus and Ausonius, to German history, but there can be no doubt of the gain to scholarship in general.

As to the personnel, there were losses and gains, but the latter preponderated. Pertz's last group, Scheffer-Boichorst, Arndt and Weiland all left to take chairs. Into their places came recruits of note: Heller, an attractive character who died young in 1880; Holder-Egger,[2] a pupil of Waitz who was to equal and perhaps surpass his master in critical genius, and who remained a loyal Monumentist from his student days till his death; Bruno Krusch,[3]

---

[1] As Sickel himself recounted (*Bresslau*, p. 531), the members of the directorate, though complimentary, clearly failed to make sense of his Latin.

[2] 1851–1911. See *A.D.B.*, Wattenbach in *N.A.*, VI, pp. 456ff., and he memoir by K. Zeumer in *N.A.*, XXXVI, pp. 821ff.

[3] 1857–1940.

another faithful worker; Harry Bresslau,[1] eminent
alike as palaeographer, editor and historian; Felix
Liebermann, familiar to English historians for his
work on Old English and Norman law and constitution; Ludwig Traube,[2] the great textual scholar. The
output of the years after 1875 was as notable for
quantity as for quality. In the *Scriptores* alone six
folios, three quartos and eighteen octavo volumes
appeared. Meanwhile the *Laws*, divided into five
subsections, made good progress under Karl Zeumer
and Friedrich Thaner; in the *Diplomata* Sickel, having eliminated Karl Pertz, recruited among others
the illustrious Paul Kehr; in the *Letters* Wattenbach
secured the brilliant young Paul Ewald for the letters
of Gregory the Great, and it was Ewald who introduced to the learned world the rich collection of
papal letters from the British Museum supplied by
Edmund Bishop. In the *Antiquities* Dümmler, with
the aid of Max Manitius and above all of Traube,
produced an excellent series of editions of Latin
medieval poetry. Yet another innovation was the
change of the old, dull and reticent periodical or
Archiv of the Society into the *Neues Archiv*, which
under the energetic editorship of Wattenbach became
one of the leading learned journals of Europe, with
articles and studies bearing on the *Monumenta*, a

---

[1] 1848–1926. Bresslau was professor-extraordinary at Berlin, 1877–90,
professor at Strasbourg, 1890–1918, and at Heidelberg for the remainder
of his life. Memoir by Kehr in *N.A.*, XLVII, pp. 251ff. See also his autobiographical contribution (n. 2) to *Die Geschichtswissenschaft der Gegen-
wart in Selbstdarstellungen*, II, (1926).

[2] 1861–1907. *N.A.*, XXXIII, pp. 539ff.; P. Lehmann, introductory
memoir to Traube's *Vorlesungen* (Munich 1909), I.

chronicle and forecast of its activities, and notices of literature bearing upon it.

Waitz died, at the height of his powers, on 25 May 1886. Ranke had preceded him by twenty-four hours, and on his death-bed had inquired how his most brilliant and faithful pupil did.[1] Waitz was not only the greatest of German medievalists and a firm leader; he was also a man of singular loyalty and integrity whom all respected as deeply as they admired him. Alike by his energy, his wisdom, his foresight and his personal relations he had rebuilt the *Monumenta*.

The relatively sudden disappearance of Waitz left the succession in the air. Wattenbach was elected acting-president; he had probably been Waitz's choice, and it was assumed by himself and many others that he would succeed without dispute, but in fact a vexatious controversy arose. The directorate was autonomous, with no subordination to the ministry, but the *Monumenta* was financed by the government and Waitz's salary had been paid to the person not to his office. In these circumstances it was natural that the ministry should seize every chance to get control of the appointment, and the executive committee of Berlin academics, rent, so it has been suggested, by domestic and foreign rivalries, and dominated by Mommsen, a master-schemer, agreed somewhat hastily that the directorate should do no more than present for nomination by the

---

[1] See *Abhandlungen d. preussischen Akademie d. Wissenschaften* (1886), p. 3: 'Was macht denn der treue Waitz?' The words quoted by Wattenbach are also in Eberhard Waitz's memoir, p. 79.

Kaiser. This might have been a harmless concession, but when they proceeded to elect, opinion was fatally and firmly divided, and Wattenbach and Dümmler received an equal number (7) of votes. This produced an unfortunate deadlock. We need not examine the complicated and painful details of the controversy, which in its progressive stages weakened ever more the position of the directorate *vis-à-vis* the government; in the course of months both Wattenbach and Dümmler refused to stand and then cancelled their refusal. In 1887 it was decided to choose two names for presentation to the government; though the composition of the directorate had changed somewhat the voting resulted as before in a tie; and the government appointed Dümmler. This unfortunate affair had two results; it deprived the directorate of its freedom of election of the president; and it occasioned a change of statute by which the president, no longer necessarily a member of the directorate or in charge of *Scriptores*, was made a full-time director; it was the first step towards an institute.

Once appointed, Dümmler showed himself a tactful, kindly and energetic chief, who gradually healed the wounds of battle. He secured yet another considerable increase in the grant and more commodious rooms for the *Monumenta* and its meetings. Of more questionable wisdom was his achievement in securing the appointment of Holder-Egger with a good salary as assistant director with a seat on the directorate; it was another tap on the wedge of government control. In the realm of editorial policy Dümmler of set purpose maintained the tradition of

Waitz, and his term of office, 1887–1902, is therefore the second half of a single epoch, though Dümmler was a less forceful personality than Waitz, and allowed the autonomy of the sections to become almost a constitutional doctrine. Since Wattenbach had resigned and persisted in his withdrawal, the *Scriptores* (which he had held since Waitz's death) and the *Neues Archiv* required new leaders; Holder-Egger took over the folio *Scriptores*; Bresslau the *Neues Archiv*. Mommsen, now a septuagenarian, continued his astounding career of productivity and among other work published his great edition of Cassiodorus (1894) and the edition of the *Liber Pontificalis* (1898) which rivalled, but did not supplant, that of Duchesne. Among notable recruits were Tangl,[1] Wilhelm Levison,[2] Alfons Dopsch and Hermann Bloch; among birds of passage the great Wilamowitz-Möllendorf and Heinrich Böhmer, who left his mark on so many diverse subjects. Other memorable achievements of the Dümmler regime were the series of critical lives of the Merovingian saints by Krusch and Levison, which impinged upon Bollandist preserves, the editions by Dümmler and others of the Carolingian letter-writers such as Alcuin, Lupus of Ferrières and Paschasius Radbert, and the masterly edition, not completed for several decades, of Salimbene by Holder-Egger. In a place apart stand the three additional volumes of quarto

---

[1] 1861–1920. Memoir by P. Kehr in *N.A.*, XLIV, pp. 139ff.

[2] 1876–1947. An exile from Nazi Germany, he was received as a guest professor at Durham University, and in 1943 delivered the Ford Lectures at Oxford on the Anglo-Saxon church.

Scriptores, originally planned by Waitz, and entitled *Libelli de Lite*, being treatises and letters connected with the great contest—always the 'lis' *antonomastice* to German historians—between Empire and Papacy. Finally, no account of this time would be complete without mention of Bresslau's classical textbook on medieval diplomatic[1] which, among other things, standardized the method, devised by Sickel, of counterchecking collation by dictation of the script against the original.

Dümmler died in harness in 1902; a few weeks before his death Mommsen, now 85, had retired from his editorial work. Strangely and unfortunately, Dümmler's death gave rise to another contretemps similar to and even more disastrous than that of 1886. This time the government was smartly off the mark and forestalled independent action by appointing Holder-Egger as *locum tenens* pending the election of a president; this *fait accompli* was accepted, and the presentation of names deferred till 1903. Once again opinion was sharply divided. To some Bresslau seemed to have a strong claim, by reason of his great services to the *Monumenta* and his vivacious and likable personality. He was, however, a Jew, and had never been *persona grata* in Berlin. Holder-Egger, on the other hand, though unrivalled as an editor, was neither a scholar of width nor a leader of men, and old Mommsen, active as ever though on the verge of the grave, was against him. After much complicated manoeuvring, in a badly arranged vote for first preference Holder-Egger alone came

[1] His *Handbuch d. Urkundenlehre* was first published in 1889.

out with a clear majority. As the Minister had asked
for three names at least, it was decided to add three
unlikely and even recalcitrant candidates in order to
force in Holder-Egger; this deprived Bresslau of any
chances he might have had on a straight vote, and
he felt the blow deeply. Nor in fact did the trick
come off. The government, who would have none of
Holder-Egger, held up the appointment and decided
to reorganize the *Monumenta* once again as a state-
controlled institute, directed, if need be, by an
administrator who was not a medievalist. Delays
and hitches of all kinds supervened, and for four
years the *Monumenta* lay in the doldrums. This
delay accentuated the weakness and the fissiparous
tendencies of the fabric; editors delayed, prevaricated
and defaulted; individual scholars indulged their
taste for luxuriant indices and apparatus; a number
of bad choices were made, both of texts to edit and
of editors to do the work; some faulty editions
appeared, especially in the *Laws*, and were mangled
by the critical wolves, some of them in the sheep's
clothing of Monumentists. Without an effective head
there was a real danger that all the channels of movement would silt up; to use another metaphor, it
needed firm central direction to keep all the balls in
the air at once.

At last, in July 1906, the government nominated
Reinhold Koser, the distinguished historian of
Frederick the Great, now for ten years head of the
Prussian State Archives. It was another step towards
the institute, another step away from the old con-
ception of the chairmanship of a technical medievalist,

primus inter pares, and both Holder-Egger and Bresslau were wounded. Koser, however, was a good administrator and an almost too tactful colleague. He did much to improve the status of the young workers, and took the first steps towards integrating them into the academic ladders of seniority, though by securing two state-paid posts he advanced another step towards bureaucracy.

Meanwhile Traube had died in 1907, and his great collection of books was bought by friends and presented to the *Monumenta*. Holder-Egger died in 1911 and was succeeded in the *Scriptores* by Bresslau; among notable publications were Levison's Life of Boniface (1905) and the Anglo-Saxon saints (1919–20), Ehwald's Aldhelm (1913–19), Tangl's Letters of Boniface (1916) and Caspar's Register of Gregory VII. Nevertheless, the *Monumenta* was not in the best of health. It was now operating in three distinct centres —the directorate and several sections at Berlin, the Carolingian *Diplomata* at Vienna, and the *Scriptores* and the Swabian *Diplomata* with Bresslau at Strasbourg; in all the sections the work was largely done by the disciples of the professor in charge of the section, and there was a tendency, already seen on a high level in Holder-Egger, for the Monumentist to be a technician rather than a medieval historian.

Koser died shortly after the outbreak of war in 1914, and for some years Bresslau held the fort. But he was once more deprived, partly now by age but chiefly from unwillingness to leave Strasbourg, of the final distinction of the presidency, and in 1919, when Germany's fortunes were at their nadir, Paul

Kehr,[1] a pupil of Sickel who had long since done work for the *Monumenta* and who had in 1915 succeeded Koser as Director of the Prussian State Archives, was nominated and confirmed—the only time, as he himself wryly remarked, that the directorate had voted unanimously. Kehr was by temperament an autocrat and a realist, some might say a pragmatist. He had little sympathy with the liberal views of Bresslau and others,[2] but he did the *Monumenta* an inestimable service in the years after 1919 and in the crisis of inflation. He restored the finances, shifted it to new and convenient quarters in a wing of the building of the State Library, and reorganized the work in three sections with full-time directors: *Scriptores*, *Leges* and *Diplomata*. Of these he took over the last and himself edited three volumes of Carolingian charters. Kehr was still in command when the regime of Hitler gripped Germany. He was not a Nazi, but his realistic, agnostic, authoritarian frame of mind allowed him to go part of the way, at least, with the tide. In 1934 a decree of the Minister of the Interior announced the take-over of the *Monumenta*, and on 1 April 1935 a remarkably

[1] 1860–1944. Memoir by W. Holtzmann in *D.A.*, VIII, pp. 26ff. Kehr's great work as a scholar was to initiate and organize a complete collection, country by country, of papal documents. Among his collaborators Walther Holtzmann, himself a Monumentist since 1946, has published three volumes of *Papsturkunden in England*.

[2] Kehr wrote of Bresslau's liberalism (*N.A.*, XLVII, p. 266): 'Dass dies alles Doktorfragen seien und dass es vielmehr auf die Praxis, auf die Wirklichkeit und auf die Loyalität der leitenden Persönlichkeiten ankomme, wollte er wenigstens theoretisch nicht zugeben.' But would the loyalty of leading persons have saved Bresslau, the Jew, from crossing the Rhine again in the opposite direction had he lived ten years longer?

laconic communiqué promulgated a new constitution.[1] According to this, the *Monumenta* became a Reichsinstitut directly under the Minister, who had the appointment of the director. The old directorate was changed into a council of twelve honorary members appointed by the Minister with a merely consultative function. At the same time the *Neues Archiv*, after a break, became the *Deutsches Archiv* (1937). Kehr accepted the change, but retired in the following year. He was succeeded as president by E. E. Strengel (1937–42) and Th. Mayer (1942–5).

The *Monumenta* continued to function during the first four years of the war, but when the Allied air offensive showed signs of developing the president and his assistants removed to a mansion near Bamberg put at their disposal by the owner, while the more precious of the collections were stored in the galleries of a mine.[2] At the end of the war the Bavarian government came to the rescue of the finances, but the losses were very serious. The documents in the mine had been burnt by a gang of foreign workers, and the stock of printed volumes at Weidmann's had been destroyed by enemy action. The president, Mayer, was *persona non grata* to the Allies, and he was replaced by W. Goetz, the true saviour of the *Monumenta*. Finally, under F. Baethgen (1947–58) the *Monumenta* was reorganized once more. Head-

---

[1] For an account of this, see P. Kehr, 'Die preussische Akademie und die *M.G.H.*,' in *Sitzungsberichte der preussischen Akademie der Wissenschaften*, phil.-hist. Kl. (1935), pp. 740–77. The 'Bericht über die Herausgabe der *M.G.H.*' in 1934 is ibid., p. 731. The statutes of 1935 are ibid., and in *D.A.*, I (1937) p. 276.

[2] For this, see *D.A.*, VIII (1950), pp. 1ff.

quarters were established at Munich of the 'Deutsches Institut für Erforschung des Mittelalters.' The constitutions were in large part identical with those in force before 1935, but the president was to be freely elected by the directorate for presentation to the Bavarian Minister of Education.[1] The directorate itself was to contain two members from the five German academies of Berlin, Munich, Göttingen, Leipzig and Heidelberg, together with two from Vienna and other scholars of note. Thus once more independent in essentials, but recognized as a state institute and with a wider field of reference, the *Monumenta* has opened yet another phase of its career. The president elected in 1959 was H. Grundmann.

The great and unique achievement of the *Monumenta* has been to realize Stein's ambition of presenting Germans, or at least German historians, with an almost complete library of the literary and diplomatic sources of their country's history from the earliest times to the opening of the fourteenth century. The back of the task was broken by Pertz; and it must be his lasting claim to gratitude that by the sixties of the last century the materials for medieval German history were in large measure in print; this fact not only moulded the course of German historiography for more than half a century, but gave German medievalists the lead among European historians which even two disastrous wars have not taken from them.

In addition to this, and in a way that Stein could

[1] ibid., pp. 22ff.

not have foreseen, this has been done in such a way that both text and editorial matter have attained on the whole the very highest of standards, and in so doing, have raised the standard of the whole of Western historical scholarship. While it is true that the *Monumenta* as such has never been a teaching school such as the Ecole des Chartes, it has in fact acted as a nursery of professors and archivists, and as a workshop for the perfecting of certain well-defined technical skills. Take it for all in all, it is the *Monumenta* that has set up for all Western historical scholarship the ideal of the critical text.

Moreover, in the course of their labours Monumentists have made innumerable discoveries of manuscripts in the libraries of Europe, and have thus enriched German and European medieval history to an extent that can only be fully realized by those whose expertise lies in these fields. It is true that in Pertz's day the great majority of the texts printed were of interest solely to the historian of the medieval Empire; it is for this reason that the *Monumenta* remained virtually unknown in this country in the nineteenth century, and exercised so little influence upon the editors of our Rolls Series and early Camdens. But during the last eighty years the horizons both of Monumentists and of English historians have broadened and the work of Mommsen, of Traube, of Tangl and of Levison—to name but a few—has benefited the whole commonwealth of learning.

The function of the *Monumenta* in the future is not easy to foresee. Thanks largely to its past achievement, scholars now in every country are engaged in editing medieval texts with something, at least, of the skill which the *Monumenta* has taught, and which French and Belgian scholars, in particular, have brought to new perfection. At the same time, the new interests of literary and philosophical history are demanding editions of medieval texts with which, at least hitherto, the *Monumenta* has not been concerned. But such an institution, with such a history, will never be out of place so long as the critical study of medieval history is of any concern to the inhabitants of Europe.

The Rolls Series

Owing to a dearth of source material little hitherto has been known of the early history of the Rolls Series save what is contained in the *First Report of the Commission on Public Records* (vol. 1, 3 parts, H.M.S.O., 1911), especially part 2, pp. 97–8. Recently, however, the Public Record Office documents and correspondence connected with *Chronicles and Memorials* have become available for consultation, and my thanks are due to the late Keeper of the Records, Sir David Evans, for drawing my attention to this. In this lecture I have done no more than scratch the surface; the full story remains to be written. The relevant documents are chiefly contained in the collection P.R.O. 37, where nos. 1–11 are original correspondence, 12–16 the official letter books (cited below as LB), no. 18 records of payments, and 19–21 the incoming correspondence from editors, arranged in packets alphabetically. Public Records quoted in this lecture, in which Crown Copyright is reserved, are printed by permission of the Controller of Her Majesty's Stationery Office.

4

The Rolls Series

THE publication of the *Chronicles and Memorials of Great Britain and Ireland during the Middle Ages*, known familiarly as the Rolls Series, was the outcome of a movement set on foot early in the nineteenth century by Henry Petrie. Petrie (1768–1842), who began life as a dancing-master, made himself a learned and zealous antiquary, and acquired a knowledge, unrivalled in his day, of the materials for early English history. He was patronized by the second Earl Spencer (1755–1834), then engaged upon the enrichment of Althorp library, and in 1818 a meeting of noblemen and gentlemen was convened at Spencer House to induce the government to support a scheme for printing the early sources of British history. The project was approved by the then Prime Minister, Lord Liverpool, and took shape in an humble address of the House of Commons to King George IV (25 July 1822), begging for the publication of manuscript sources of history; as a result of this, Petrie, who had been appointed Keeper of Records in the Tower of London in 1819, assembled extracts from various sources for the period before the Norman Conquest, which were published posthumously in 1848 as *Monumenta Historica Britannica*. This was a selective collection, modelled on the *Recueil* of the Maurist Dom Bouquet, which

Guizot had continued in France. Petrie's *Monumenta* was inordinately costly, while it failed to give real satisfaction to historians.

Meanwhile a lengthy attempt had been made to assemble, safeguard and publish administrative and other records of the English past, which had long been recognized as constituting a collection without rival in Europe. The effort at first took two directions: the establishment under the Public Record Office Act of 1838 of a great depository, and the inauguration of a series of Record and State Papers Commissions, of which the last expired in 1848, having published *inter alia* an edition of Rymer's *Foedera* and *Statutes of the Realm*, with a selection of *State Papers*. These Commissions, also, had been exorbitantly expensive, and could show comparatively little for their outlay of £260,000.[1]

In the fifth decade of the century these two streams of publication, the historical and the record, were united in the person of Thomas Hardy, Petrie's pupil at the Tower, and a diligent editor for the Record Commission. He was already sufficiently well known to be one of those considered for the post of Deputy Keeper of the Records (D.K.), when the Public Record Office came into being in 1838 under the supervision of the Master of the Rolls (M.R.), with a staff of clerks and workers. This establishment

[1] For all this the *First Report* may serve as a starting-point, especially pt 2, pp. 1–17, 26, 75–114. cf. also C. P. Cooper, *An account of the most important Public Records of Great Britain* (Record Commission, 2 vols., 1832). See also the introduction to T. D. Hardy's *Descriptive Catalogue of Materials relating to the History of Great Britain and Ireland* (R.S., 1862–71), I, pp. xlvi ff.

owed much to the energy and foresight of Henry
Bickersteth, first and only Lord Langdale, who was
its first head. Lord Langdale, whose bust confronts
every visitor to the search rooms, and who acquired
a certain notoriety by his judgment in the *cause
célèbre* of *Gorham* v. *the Bishop of Exeter*, must
take an honourable place among those who made
the period an age of reform.[1] He was assisted with
zeal, if not always with discretion, by the first
Deputy Keeper, Sir Francis Palgrave. This scholar,
the father of four distinguished sons, one of whom,
professor of poetry at Oxford, gave us *The Golden
Treasury*, while another, in the course of an adven-
turous career, was in and out of the Society of Jesus,
deserves attention in his own right as an early-
Victorian servant of Clio.[2] By birth a Jew (his
father's name was Cohen), he followed Disraeli to
the waters of baptism and acquired a very deep and
varied learning, which he devoted to an energetic
campaign for the preservation and publication of
records. In later life he was responsible alike for the
photozincographic reproduction of Domesday Book,
and for the engagement of J. S. Brewer, a man of
many parts, to edit the Letters and Papers of
Henry VIII. Both these enthusiasts had a share in
the genesis of the Rolls Series, but the three men
to whose efforts its inception was directly due were
Sir John (later first Lord) Romilly, who succeeded
Langdale at Rolls House (1851–73), T. (later Sir

[1] T. D. Hardy, *Memoirs of the Life of Henry, Lord Langdale* (1852),
and *D.N.B.*

[2] For him and his sons, see *D.N.B.*

Thomas) Duffus Hardy, who succeeded Palgrave as D.K. (1861–78), and that estimable scholar-antiquarian, Joseph Stevenson.[1]

John Romilly (1802–74), son of Sir Samuel Romilly, statesman and Solicitor-General in the 'ministry of all the talents' (1806), had a distinguished career in parliament, being successively Solicitor-General and Attorney-General in Lord John Russell's ministry of 1848, and Master of the Rolls. Besides his other activities at the Record Office, he is remembered as having abolished the fees formerly levied upon searchers. His industry, patience, courtesy and good sense are abundantly evident in his correspondence. Thomas Duffus Hardy (1804–78), the son of an army officer, was descended from a Jersey family which had given several distinguished admirals to the Royal Navy. He himself entered the Record Office at the Tower when fifteen years old, and served for many years under Petrie; he became an expert archivist and palaeographer, and edited a series of Close, Patent, Fine, Charter and Liberate Rolls for the Record Commission. He also took a large part in the establishment of the first Historical Manuscripts Commission. Hardy was an authentic, if self-taught, scholar, and his descriptive catalogue of manuscripts, ultimately completed by his brother and C. T. Martin and printed in the Rolls Series, has helped innumerable scholars in the past and has indeed not yet been wholly superseded. His correspondence shows him

[1] For these, see *D.N.B.*, and for Stevenson also the memoir by J. H. Pollen in *The Month* (May 1895).

as a judicious, upright, loyal man, whom all respected,
though there are few traces of any warmer feeling.
The third of the trio, Joseph Stevenson (1806–95),
played many parts in the course of his long life. Born
at Berwick and schooled at Durham under James
Raine the elder, he at first prepared himself for the
presbyterian ministry, but changed his mind and
accepted a post in the British Museum, where he
worked upon the edition of Rymer's *Foedera*. He
then joined the established church, was ordained
and appointed librarian to the dean and chapter of
Durham in succession to Raine, but left in 1849 to
become the vicar of Leighton Buzzard. There he
began a great chronological catalogue of English
historical writers and their manuscripts for the
Clarendon Press; this was later embodied by Hardy
in his *Descriptive Catalogue*. It was at this time,
also, that he took his share in the genesis of the
Rolls Series. Meanwhile he had begun to feel doubts
as to his position as an Anglican and resigned his
benefice, accepting soon after employment in the
Record Office, and in 1863 was received into
the Catholic Church. The Record Office was at the
moment having trouble with the Protestant Alliance,
and though both Romilly and Hardy supported him,
Stevenson was edged out and retired to Birmingham,
where he worked for the Historical Manuscripts
Commission. When his wife died in 1869 he studied
for the priesthood at Oscott and was ordained by
Bishop Ullathorne in 1872. In the same year
Mr Gladstone, advised by Romilly, Hardy, Brewer
and Lord Acton, was broad-minded enough to

award him a small pension on the civil list, which he used for several years in making transcripts of English documents in the Vatican Library. In 1877 he entered the Society of Jesus, and became an honoured member of that body, continuing his historical studies at Farm Street till his death in 1895.

The number of medieval texts edited or translated by Stevenson in a working life of sixty years was truly remarkable, and others besides myself may have taken some time to realize that the *Chronica de Mailros* (1835), the *Chronicon de Abingdon* (1858), the *Chronicon Anglicanum* of Ralph of Coggeshall (1875) and the *Life of Jane Dormer* (1887) were all the work of a single writer. Stevenson's letters make up by far the largest of the bundles of T. D. Hardy's correspondence. There was a real warmth of feeling and intimacy between them, and Stevenson was alone in subscribing himself 'yours affectionately' to the D.K. and addressing him as 'old fellow.' The last and one of the most learned of the self-taught editors, he lived on into the age of Stubbs and Tout, and it is to his initiative, in the last resort, that we owe the Rolls Series.

Stevenson, Brewer and Hardy had together in 1848 pressed for the publication of historical sources without effect. On 29 November 1856 the vicar of Leighton Buzzard wrote again, taking the parliamentary report of 1832 as his text. His letter, addressed to the Permanent Under-Secretary of the Treasury, Sir Charles Trevelyan, brother-in-law to Lord Macaulay, suggested that the publication of a series of pre-Reformation sources of English history would be a desirable enterprise. He drew attention to Guizot's activity in France, and that of the Monumentists in Germany, and, after noting that Hardy and Brewer were occupied with other important tasks, offered to undertake the work of organizing the series himself.[1]

Trevelyan duly passed the letter to the M.R. Romilly took almost eight weeks to acknowledge it, but his reply, when it came (26 January 1857), was all that could be wished. No doubt the M.R. had taken counsel with Hardy, but his long letter was unmistakably his own.[2] After remarking that England, 'alone amongst Governments of modern civilized nations,' had 'taken no steps to produce their historical treasures,' he proceeded to discuss at length what should be published, in what manner, by whom and by whose authority. He then gave an admirable analysis of the various classes of documents and the best way of publication. He set aside Stevenson's offer to edit a representative collection, and recommended the employment of separate editors of texts, to be chosen and invited by the M.R. under the surveillance of the Lords of the Treasury. As for expense, £3,000 a year for ten years would, he thought, see the thing through. On 10 February 1857 Trevelyan, on behalf of the Treasury, accepted the scheme almost unchanged, and after further discussion

[1] P.R.O. 37/12 (i.e. LB, 1), pp. 14–20. I give references to the LB, when available, as being the simplest direction. In many cases the original letters can also be seen in the accompanying bundles.

[2] LB, 1, pp. 21–56.

Romilly requested Sir Francis Palgrave, D.K., Brewer, Hardy and Stevenson to furnish him with a list of works to be printed.[1]

Palgrave, when asked, could only suggest the Books of the Corporation of London, which contained, so he said, interesting information on every kind of topic, such as the medieval use of oil in painting and the technique of making puff pastry. 'These books,' he added, 'should be considered the fore-horse of our team . . . There is no subject (not even those which lend themselves to religious controversy) equally interesting.' Brewer was more practical, and listed some eighty texts, of which a majority duly appeared in the Rolls Series. Hardy, for his part, gave a list of sixty-five works, many of them duplicating Brewer and almost all printed sooner or later in the series. As for Stevenson, he gave a shorter list, agreeing in the main with Brewer and Hardy, but giving emphasis to letters, councils and papal bulls.

At a second meeting of Palgrave, Hardy and Brewer at Rolls House, on 28 February, letters of support and offers of help were ready.[2] Palgrave tended to disagree with his colleagues, and in fact seems to have taken no further part in the enterprise. Brewer's proposals, with additions from Hardy, were considered anew, and a short list drawn up. Within the next fortnight invitations were sent out and offers accepted, and on 15 April a list of the first fourteen volumes was available—a mixed grill, including Brewer's *Adam Marsh*, Luard's *Lives of Edward the*

---

[1] LB, I, p. 62.   [2] ibid., pp. 74–6.

Confessor, J. E. B. Mayor's *Richard of Cirencester*, Gairdner's *Chronicles of Henry VII*, together with some very slow starters and the two volumes of Capgrave by Hingeston that were to be the beginning of sorrows for Romilly.[1] On 1 June the Chancellor and the M.R. agreed on printing 1,500 copies, and on 9 June the printing order was taken to the Stationery Office.[2]

We may allow that the M.R. had done a remarkably brisk piece of work. Six months from the receipt of Stevenson's letter he had squared the Exchequer, made all financial and technical arrangements and started up a dozen editors on an ample agreed programme. His biographer tells us that as a judge Romilly was hard-working and expeditious, but that the rapidity of his decision sometimes led to a reversal of his judgments on appeal; he adds that 'perhaps his example of rapid decision was worth more than the cost of his errors.'[3] A similar judgment might be passed on him as director of the *Chronicles and Memorials*, with the additional comment that in all probability no other M.R. of the century would have acted with equal decision and sound sense. The framework established by him was maintained in its main lines to the end, though none of his successors took an active personal share in the work. The sole authority was the M.R. He invited or accepted editors, rejected or approved their choice of material and gave them 'employment,' but each

---

[1] ibid., pp. 100–02.
[2] ibid., pp. 112–14.
[3] *D.N.B.*, XLIX, p. 187.

proposal was referred to the Treasury for confirmation, and their Lordships remained always in the
background to solve difficulties by an anonymous
non possumus. The individual editor was given complete freedom and bore sole responsibility, but in
practice Romilly and successive D.K.s advised on all
technical matters and whipped up the stragglers. The
rate of pay to the editors was fixed at eight guineas
per sheet of sixteen pages, but if smaller type preponderated the rate might rise to twelve guineas. The
editor had to bear all expenses, including fees to
copyists, but on occasion fees for transcripts of
distant manuscripts were refunded. The average
size of a volume was fixed at 500 pages, including
the introduction. The initial grant of £2,000 in
1857–8 was raised to £3,000 in the following year,
and stood at this level till 1867–8, when it fell back
to £2,000, where it stood till the eighties.[1] The
whole grant was, however, available for the editors'
fees, as the printing costs fell entirely on the
Stationery Office.

In early days many offers, desirable and undesir-
able, reached the M.R. and the D.K., ranging from
that of a Welsh printer's compositor, who had bardic
qualifications and volunteered to do translations
from the Cymric, to that of Sir Thomas Phillipps, who
begged for the publication of Pipe Rolls and Feet of
Fines, only to be told that the M.R. had no authority
to print records.[2] On 27 March Dr J. A. Giles

---

[1] P.R.O. 37/18. The figures cited occur on the early pages, which are
not numbered. In 1880–1 the grant was still £2,000 but it decreased
shortly after this date.

[2] LB, I, p. 81 (27 Feb.).

solicited employment, endeavouring to remove prejudice by the admission that in the past, owing to financial stringency, he had been 'content to transfer many MSS. to print without that [*sic*] minutiae of criticism which Bentley and Porson employed.' He was not, however, engaged.[1] A few days later Hardy received the following letter:

April 1st, 1857   Navestock,
                                          Romford.

    My dear Sir,
    I have just heard that the government are going to print some of the early English histories—I do not know how far this is correct, but if it is, I am anxious to offer my services as an Editor of any such publications as they may contemplate. I apply to you, as I imagine you are the most likely person to have information on the matter. I am afraid that my never having published anything on the subject and not being known as a student of English history may hinder my being accepted in such a position, but that I cannot help. I was a first class in classics at Oxford in 1848 and Fellow of Trinity College, and have for years devoted myself to this particular study. Would you kindly let me know what is the best thing to do to be accepted, and excuse this hurried note. You may remember me as having bothered you once or twice at the Record Office about bishops.
                    I am,
              Yours very sincerely,
              William Stubbs.

    The letter book records that 'Mr Hardy answered this letter and declined Mr Stubbs' proposition.'[2]

---

[1] LB, II, pp. 98 (27 Mar.), 104 (16 Apr.).
[2] LB, I, pp. 98 (1 Apr.), 139 (9 Feb. 1858), 142 (17 Feb.); LB, II, p. 33.

Stubbs refused to take no for an answer and wrote twice again in subsequent years. On the third occasion Hardy wrote to the M.R.:

> This is the third application Mr Stubbs has made for employment, and has not as yet done anything to show that he is competent to edit such works as he has proposed, but it does not follow that he is incompetent. He is generally employed as an assistant to others, and is considered a safe and accurate person.[1]

The M.R., however, again turned Stubbs down, and it was not till 1862 that he got home on a fourth application. Four years later he was Regius professor.[2]

The two first volumes appeared in February 1858. One of them, appropriately enough, was Stevenson's *Historia Abbendonensis*, a useful but uncritical piece of work. The other was Capgrave's *Historia de Illustribus Henricis*, edited by the Rev. Mr F. C. Hingeston, and with its publication began what is perhaps the most distressing episode in the history of the series. Hingeston, a young Fellow of Exeter College, had been recommended by Stevenson, and the correspondence shows him visiting Leighton Buzzard as the accepted suitor of Stevenson's eldest daughter, a circumstance that may have affected the older man's judgment. He was a self-confident, naïve, mercurial young man, and a tireless and copious correspondent. His first assignment, two works of Capgrave, was an easy task with an autograph manuscript in each case.

---

[1] Manuscript note by T. D. Hardy in P.R.O. 37/61.

[2] For the circumstances of Stubbs's appointment to the Regius chair, see N. J. Williams, *Bulletin of the Institute of Historical Research*, XXXIII (May 1960), pp. 121–5.

The reviewers, however, were unfavourable and, as Hardy observed, the first volume 'produced general disappointment.' The second was out in November; in it he 'disappointed the world more than in his former work.' He had, it transpired, used Petrie's transcript of the autograph, and had made no attempt to check its many inaccuracies. Nevertheless, he was commissioned to edit a collection of royal and historical letters of the reign of Henry IV, in two volumes.[1] The first duly appeared in 1860, to be received very coolly. The material was badly selected, and Hingeston had taken no trouble to produce a correct text, either of the Latin, the French or the English. A long and painful correspondence with Romilly ensued. Whether or not the editor had hoped to ensure a permanent source of income, the matter selected for publication was so voluminous that one volume covered only six years, and the M.R. pointed out that the undertaking as planned on this scale would run to thirty volumes.[2] Meanwhile Hingeston, on the crest of the wave, had been tactless enough in 1860 to throw over Stevenson's daughter, and the outraged father took it very ill.[3] A long

---

[1] LB, I, pp. 195, 254, 258, 263–4; LB, II, pp. 91–3. The M.R. had congratulated Hingeston when the first volume of Capgrave appeared (P.R.O. 37/44, 3 Feb. 1858).

[2] LB, I, pp. 253–4 (7 Mar. 1860).

[3] Stevenson's letters in P.R.O. 37/59: (1 May 1858) 'His conduct has proved him base, treacherous and untruthful to a degree which I could not have credited but for proofs too ample and convincing to be disputed'; (4 May) 'The prevailing feeling of my mind is thankfulness that my child did not become the wife of one who has proved himself so utterly unworthy of her'; (No date, probably referring to Hingeston) 'I had not seen the marriage of which you speak, and am afraid I could not congratulate the Lady did I know her.'

silence followed, and when next heard of Hingeston holds the living of Ringdown near Ivybridge in S. Devon, and is pressing for a payment on account and inviting Hardy to visit him and enjoy the sea-bathing.[1] Meanwhile, on the expectation of plenty, he had pledged some £200 partly to a local builder and partly towards an organ in his church.[2] When at last, on 2 October 1864, the second volume was in type the M.R. himself looked it over and, misliking what he saw, commissioned Riley and Brewer to recollate the manuscripts and check the translation.[3] The result of their work, which is still extant,[4] was decisive. Though Hingeston agreed to make most of the required changes, the sight of the volume, with the editor's modest list of six errata followed by sixteen supplementary pages filled to the brim by his critics, to say nothing of the cancellation marks on sixty-two pages of text, was too much for Romilly, and the volume was suppressed.[5] Eight copies were preserved as a literary curiosity; the rest of the edition was pulped. That was the end of Hingeston's connection with the Rolls Series, but under the longer version of Hingeston-Randolph his name is kept in memory, if not in benediction, by students of the Exeter episcopal registers.

Meanwhile Romilly had been suffering from

[1] P.R.O. 37/44. The reference to bathing occurs in a letter of 30 Dec. 1863.

[2] ibid., letter of 5 Oct. 1864. The organ cost £120.

[3] LB, II, pp. 287-92 (15 Dec. 1864), 284-5 (17 Nov. 1864).

[4] P.R.O. 37/4.

[5] LB, II, pp. 287-92. The Public Record Office has a copy of the suppressed volume.

Benjamin Thorpe.[1] Thorpe had been among the first to apply for employment, and had given 'much pain' to the M.R. by blaming Hardy's personal enmity for the rebuff he had suffered. On 6 May 1858 the Anglo-Saxon Chronicle was assigned to him, and a year later the proofs were coming in. Romilly, rendered suspicious by a glance at Petrie's text in the *Monumenta Britannica*, asked Thorpe if he had collated his manuscripts. Thorpe replied in the negative; he had followed Petrie. This gave Romilly 'very great pain mingled with some apprehension,' neither of which emotions was lessened when he collated Thorpe's text with facsimiles of the manuscript. He therefore stopped the printing (21 April 1860) and a long wrangle ensued between the old and infirm editor and the M.R., who somewhat unreasonably refused to accept any collation of the Cambridge manuscript save that of Thorpe himself. In the end thirteen sheets were cancelled and Thorpe mulcted accordingly before the edition appeared—a valuable production, although replaced within thirty years by the work of Earle and Plummer.

While Thorpe was still on the tapis Romilly was at odds with no less a person than the aged Sir Henry Ellis, whose edition of Oxenedes abounded in errors of transcription, blunders and misprints of every kind.[2]

[1] For Thorpe, see the somewhat indulgent article by T. Seccombe in *D.N.B.*, and LB, I, pp. 147 (7 Mar. 1858), 211, 212–17, 222, 232 (where Romilly goes to the British Museum 'for a couple of hours'); LB, II, pp. 37–9, 67.

[2] P.R.O. 37/59 (undated letter of Stevenson): 'I cannot tell you how shocked I am with poor old Ellis's book. It is bad beyond credibility, you need to see it in order to understand the amount and grossness of the errors.'

On this occasion the M.R. himself went down
to the Museum and did some collating, as a result of
which the volume was cancelled and R. B. Knowles
employed to collate the whole work again.[1] This
gentleman, then employed by the Record Office, had
earned a niche for himself as a playwright and
journalist. He subsequently applied for employment
as editor, but was rejected by the Lords of the
Treasury, who fought shy of 'a gentleman of the
Roman Catholic persuasion.' There was a history
behind this. The Record Office had recently suffered
unwelcome publicity at the hands of the Protestant
Alliance. One of its employees, W. B. Turnbull, had
become a Catholic and had not only been forced by
a press campaign into resignation, but had been
pursued by the Protestant Alliance with the accusa-
tion of having removed valuable documents of
national importance. The Lords of the Treasury,
therefore, were taking no chances, but it is pleasant
to find both Hardy and Romilly fighting, if vainly,
on the side of tolerance and good sense.[2]

These and other lesser troubles of the kind were
a source of anxiety at the time, and have permanently
impaired the repute of the Rolls Series, but they must
not be allowed to obscure the mass of useful and
excellent work that was being done. Romilly and

---

[1] LB, I, p. 238, and for the cancellation LB, II, pp. 75-6. The
employment of Knowles is not acknowledged on the title-page or in the
correspondence, for obvious reasons, but the sum of £193 14s od 'for
collation' is credited to him in the Payments Book (P.R.O. 37/18, p. 31)
for 1860-1.

[2] For this, see LB, II, pp. 95-6, 127-9, and article on Turnbull in
D.N.B. Stevenson's letters contain several references to the episode.

Hardy, D.K. since 1861, must be given credit for both energy and financial ability. After less than five years (9 February 1861) the M.R. could report that 28 volumes had already been published, with 9 others in the press and 4 more in progress. Four years later (1 February 1865) 57 volumes were out, and in five years again (7 February 1870) the total had reached 100.[1] All this had been secured well within the limits of the grant. Despite a few fiascos and a number of ill-chosen or poorly executed volumes, several able scholars had become entrenched, among whom were two or three of very high quality. Among these William Stubbs was in a class by himself. During twenty-seven years he edited a dozen important texts accurately and speedily, and as his confidence grew he allowed himself (and was permitted) more and more space in which to discuss his author and his period in essays which rank among his most valuable historical writings.

Others also worked hard and well. H. R. Luard, Fellow of Trinity and Registrary of Cambridge University, was reliable and prolific over thirty years, and besides Hardy himself and Stevenson, Sir F. Madden, J. S. Brewer, James Gairdner, Sir E. Maunde Thompson and Canon J. C. Robertson made sound and useful contributions. The most fruitful years were those in which Hardy was D.K. under Romilly, and one who peruses the letter books and miscellaneous correspondence of those years comes to admire the industry, just dealing and wisdom of the two men. Neither of them allowed

---

[1] LB, II, pp. 44, 306; LB, III, p. 69.

himself or his editors to forget the relationship of
'employed' to employer, sharp reminders were sent
out (usually without effect) to laggards, and requests
for payments on account or augmentations of the
fee often received short shrift, but the advice given
was almost always sympathetic and practical. Particularly is this true of Romilly, who took his duties
very seriously and was prepared to write courteously
and at length to editors from his London address
and from his Herefordshire home as well as from
Rolls House. His successor, Sir George Jessel, was
less interested in the work and left most of it to his
D.K. When T. D. Hardy died in 1878 he was succeeded by his brother William, who had shared his
career and interests, though with a more limited
knowledge and a less robust personality. He retired
in 1886 and was succeeded by H. C. Maxwell Lyte,[1]
who had not previously been on the staff of the
Office. Lyte was destined to hold office for forty
years, to supervise the building of a great part of
the Public Record Office, and to inaugurate a
brilliant new period of record publications. He had
no great love for the Rolls Series, and was determined
to tidy up his inheritance with a new broom. His
greatest obstacle was the affair of the Orkney Sagas,
perhaps the quaintest of the imbroglios of the Rolls
Series. The two actors in this complicated story were
Dr (later Sir George) Dasent and Dr G. Vígfússon.
    G. Dasent (1817–96) was a more considerable

---

[1] For Maxwell Lyte, see the biographical sketches by C. Johnson
(*Proceedings of the British Academy*, XXXVI (1940)), V. H. Galbraith
(*D.N.B.* Supplement, 1931–40).

figure than the letters of the D.K. would suggest.[1] A diplomatic connection at Stockholm in early years had bred in him an interest in Norse literature, which was encouraged by Jacob Grimm, and he rapidly became a leading Scandinavian scholar and the author of numerous translations of the sagas, some of which are still in print. He was also the lifelong friend of John Delane, whose sister he married, and he was for many years assistant editor of *The Times*, a post which he combined with a chair of English literature and modern history at King's College, London. Gladstone appointed him in 1870 to the Civil Service Commission, of which he later became chief, and in 1876 Disraeli proposed him for knighthood. He was an active member of the Historical Manuscripts Commission, and moved freely in London society, both literary and political.

Gúdbrandr Vígfússon (1828–89),[2] an Icelander by birth, won recognition in Denmark as the first scholar to apply the methods of modern critical scholarship to the Sagas. At the invitation of Dasent he came to England to complete an Icelandic-English dictionary for the Clarendon Press, and from 1866 till his death lived at Oxford, where he was appointed reader in Icelandic in 1884.

The Dasent-Vígfússon saga (if the term be allowed) can be constructed from the voluminous correspondence as follows. Dasent was 'engaged' at his own suggestion by Romilly as early as 1859

[1] See article in *D.N.B.* (First Supplement, II).
[2] See article by F. York Powell in *D.N.B.* Sir Charles Oman (*Memoirs*, 1941) has a story that Vígfússon used to sit over York Powell in his room until he had completed his daily stint of work.

to edit a collection of sagas with an English translation.[1] After many delays, due to the editor's 'ill-
health and other unfortunate causes,' the first volume
was printed, but Dasent was informed almost immediately by Robert Lowe, then Chancellor of the
Exchequer and himself an Icelandic scholar, that a
much better manuscript existed at Copenhagen.
Vígfússon was engaged to collate this, and found
it not only better, but far fuller; it was therefore
decided to cancel the printed volume (8 May 1877)
and replace it by two containing texts by Vígfússon
and translations by Dasent.[2] The former accomplished his work speedily, the latter, who alone had
a contract with the Treasury, was again dilatory,
and Vígfússon feared that he would take both the
credit and the fee, if he did not alternatively hold up
publication indefinitely. 'The word of an Englishman,' the Icelander observed with some bitterness,
'was [once] sufficient to me, young and inexperienced
as I was . . . I was blind at the time, and knew
England only from books, a dreamland to [i.e. compared with] the England I have seen.'[3] This was in
July 1879; Dasent, for his part, complained that
Vígfússon refused to complete his short introduction,
and William Hardy got no further with the two
collaborators, each straining at the leash while waiting
for the other.

When Maxwell Lyte succeeded Hardy he broke
light-heartedly into the fray. When could Dasent get

[1] LB, I, pp. 210–11.
[2] LB, III, pp. 242–3, 261–3, 294–7, 313, 321–8, 335–41.
[3] LB, IV, p. 33; P.R.O. 37/19.

his piece done? Dasent, pleading an 'accident last autumn' (it was now May 1886) promised speedy satisfaction,[1] and the D.K. turned to Vígfússon, who now had in his pupil Frederick York Powell a loyal ally who could write better English and a clearer hand than the master. Vígfússon promised his missing pages, provided that the two volumes of text should appear in his name if Dasent prevaricated. Dasent, who had recently 'been made distracted by politics'[2] (and no wonder in 1886!), once more promised speedy execution, but a few days later was placed by Gladstone at the head of the Civil Service Commission and could, as the phrase goes, 'sit pretty,' writing on 14 August that he is 'sorry to say that my working power has been much hindered by illness in my family, which I grieve to say has now ended in death.' On 19 April 1887 Leonard Lyell, at the demand of a constituent, asked in the House what had become of the Orkney Saga. He was given the normal soothing answer,[3] but Maxwell Lyte, who had received nothing from either party, was complaining that 'each of them [Dasent and Vígfússon] has his own version of the matter, and I do not know, or wish to know, which version is correct.' W. L. Jackson of the Treasury now took a hand and visited Sir George, who was prodigal of promise but wrote on 14 June 1887 that his 'powers for work of this nature have been very much crippled by the alarming illness' of a colleague. 'I hope,' he added, 'it is no

---

[1] LB, v, p. 22, and P.R.O. 37/26.
[2] P.R.O. 37/26.
[3] LB, v, pp. 169, 174.

secret at the Treasury that the duties of this Commission are no sinecure, and that they cannot be neglected without grave injury to the Public Service.' On which Maxwell Lyte commented with acidity 'that Civil Servants entrusted with the editing of any of our Chronicles are required to do any such work' out of office hours, and he remarked upon 'the large amount of public money [some £1,200] which he [Dasent] has received for work which he has not done.'[1] No doubt the D.K. could appreciate the pensive remark of Vígfússon: 'How the time speeds away! Since 1859 twenty-eight years have ebbed away.'[2] In any case, he published the texts alone under Vígfússon's name in 1887. In March 1888 the Treasury is once more asking for news of the translations, and Maxwell Lyte is of opinion that 'Sir George Dasent has not touched the work for many years, and that he has no serious intention of ever touching it again.'[3] He adds: 'three Members of Parliament are, I believe, threatening questions about the Sagas.' This stirred the Treasury to a fresh protest (11 April) which found Sir George 'in great grief and trouble at the death of my brother,' and unable to attend to business.[4] Finally, at the end of 1889, Maxwell Lyte, remarking that 'there is a limit to my patience and that limit is almost reached,' suggested that 'failing gentler methods' the matter should be brought before the Auditor-General, thus causing Dasent to be 'cited

---

[1] ibid., pp. 201–2. Dasent had in fact done much of the work; it was his misfortune that it had been rendered useless by subsequent discoveries.
[2] ibid., pp. 190–1.
[3] ibid., pp. 276–7.
[4] LB, v, p. 281.

before the Committee of Public Accounts' for embezz-
ling public funds.[1] Within a few weeks of this
Dasent sent in his introduction and index. In the
following year his house and library were destroyed
by fire; one feels more than ordinary sympathy with
him in a calamity which only a year earlier would
have provided him with a cast-iron excuse with
which to silence his tormentors.

Dasent was not the only *damnosa hereditas* left to
Lyte by the Hardy brothers. He had also on his
hands that prince of feckless and exasperating
scholars, F. J. Furnivall. Furnivall (1825–1910),[2]
whose father, a physician, was said to have acquired
a fortune of £250,000 from a private lunatic asylum,
had lost his share of the inheritance with the failure
of Gurney's Bank in 1867, and was for the rest of his
life in straitened circumstances, which did nothing to
abate his energy or his resilience. A militant pagan
and social reformer, a brilliant Old English and
Shakespearian scholar with a wide and varied knowledge of literature, irrepressible, combative and at
times guilty of faults against good taste and manners,
he was by no means ineffective, and called forth
much good work from others; he has a secure place
in the history of English scholarship as the founder
of the Early English Text Society. He also founded
the Ballad Society, the Wyclif Society, the Browning
Society and the Shelley Society, while in another
sphere he was the father of the National Amateur
Rowing Society and the Hammersmith Sculling Club

[1] ibid., pp. 504–6 (27 Nov. 1889).
[2] *D.N.B.*

for men and women. He became one of the original Fellows of the British Academy. With such a man to handle one cannot but feel that Maxwell Lyte allowed himself to make heavy weather of an unimportant matter, and one suspects that Furnivall took an impish delight in twisting the lion's tail.

Furnivall had had the *Chronicle* of Robert of Brunne on his plate since 1860, complete now save for a short introduction. As early as 1877 T. D. Hardy had called his attention to 'the promises you have made on the [six following] dates (which you have not fulfilled).'[1] Nine years later Maxwell Lyte, then heavily engaged with Dasent, opened hostilities on another front, threatening to publish the chronicle without an introduction if one were not forthcoming by 2 August. Furnivall returned the following soft answer:

8. vii. 1886.
My dear Sir,
    All that you say of my failure to turn out Robert de Brunne's Chronicle is, alas, too true, but there is no hope whatever of my being able to complete the introduction by August 2. Just now I am good for nothing but a scull on the river, or a ride on a bicycle and marking a Shakespeare Quarto. But I'll take B.R. with me to a quiet village on the Yorkshire moors on July 20. . . . If by September 2 you can get nothing from me, then the book can go out as it is.

To this Lyte replied: 'I venture to think that this work undertaken by you for Her Majesty's Government many years ago should have precedence of all other literary studies, however interesting and attrac-

[1] LB, III, pp. 316–17.

tive.'[1] Needless to say, 2 September passed without incident, but on the 15th Furnivall wrote: 'I took all my books to Yorkshire, but never opened them. Lawn tennis, cricket, walks, picnics, getting up a Concert and Dances occupied all the holiday. Then since my return there's been the practice for our Sculling Fours race next Saturday, the arrangements for getting a Sculling Eight next season, &c.' He added, as a Trinity Hall oar to an Etonian: 'If you're an old rowing man, you should come and have a paddle in one of our Sculling Fours.'[2]

A fortnight later (1 October) another missive came. 'A disaster has befallen me. I've lost my working copy of Robert of Brunne with my half-written introduction and Mr Sweet's notes. It's an awful blow.' Then to sugar the pill he added: 'But there was one consolation. Yesterday I was told of a Clasper Eight, a £60 used only one season, to be sold for £16, out of which we can probably make a second racing Sculling Eight.'[3] Unmoved by the attractions of the river Lyte riposted (23 December 1886) that if nothing were forthcoming 'it will be with their Lordships [sc. of the Treasury] to decide whether you are still entitled to a Civil List Pension for literary services.' Furnivall answered the same day: 'Surely the threat about my pension is unworthy of you. The Pension was given me by Mr Gladstone for work quite independent of Robert of Brunne, and I think he'd be willing to justify his grant.' Unshaken,

---

[1] LB, v, p. 63; P.R.O. 37/30.   [2] P.R.O. 37/30.
[3] LB, v, pp. 89–90. Clasper was a well-known oarsman and boatbuilder.

the D.K. replied on Christmas Eve: 'I mentioned your pension, because it is not unlikely that the Lords of the Treasury may consider, as I certainly consider, that the recipient of a yearly allowance from the Civil List should be, of all persons, the last to neglect a plain duty to Her Majesty's Government.'[1] On Boxing Day Furnivall promised to do his piece; he added to his letter a P.S.: 'Had a glorious scull in a wager boat on Xmas morning. River beautiful.'[2] Six months later (22 June 1887) the introduction was sent with this note:

> My dear Sir,
> I send this at last. I have been in the country and learning to swim and sculling.
>
> Yours very truly,
> F. J. F.[3]

Dilatory editors were not the only source of trouble to the D.K. The title of the series, *Chronicles . . . of Great Britain and Ireland*, was a challenge to patriots in the north and west. As early as March 1857, J. D'Alton was demanding the inclusion of Irish material,[4] and in 1858 Romilly accepted the Rev. Williams ap Ithel as editor of the *Brut* and *Annales Cambriae*,[5] but the work was not well done. Scotland liquidated her claims by securing £1,000 for herself out of the grant to the Record

---

[1] LB, v, pp. 106–9.
[2] ibid., pp. 110–11.
[3] P.R.O. 37/30. This letter would seem to contradict the assertion in the *D.N.B.* that Furnivall never learnt to swim.
[4] LB, i, p. 90.
[5] ibid., p. 155.

Office.[1] Irish scholars kept up a dropping fire of complaints, though several Irish volumes of no very great significance were in fact published from time to time. At last, in the roaring eighties, a lively campaign was launched with a long letter in *The Times* (July 1887) from Dr Stokes, Professor of Ecclesiastical History in T.C.D. This was followed by a question from Macneill in the House, and on 8 August John Dillon, supported by T. P. O'Connor, asked for further explanation for the neglect of Ireland. 'There must,' he said, 'be some corrupt influences at work.'[2] Though the D.K. was able to prove to the minister that the complaint had no foundation, the Treasury duly authorized expenditure for one year sufficient to cover the cost of one volume, and the result was *The Cartulary of St Thomas, Dublin*, edited by J. T. Gilbert.

I have glanced at some length at these unfamiliar episodes in the archives of the Rolls Series. Others have been public property for years. The inadequacy of Sir Travers Twiss, Q.C., was exposed long ago by Stubbs and Maitland, and the stories of two of the latest additions, the one being Maitland's own *Memoranda de parliamento* and the other Hubert Hall's *Red Book of the Exchequer*, are already partly in print.[3] Maitland's volume is perhaps the most notable of the whole series, while the controversy between Hall and

---

[1] LB, IV, p. 183.   [2] LB, V, pp. 204, 214, 222.

[3] For Maitland, see the introduction by Professor Helen Cam in *Selected Essays of F. W. Maitland* (Cambridge 1957), pp. xxiv–xxvi. The Hall-Round affair gave birth to a small literature of reviews (including Round's notorious notice in *The Athenaeum*), pamphlets and letters, some of which are in the London University Library.

Horace Round is one of the classic pieces of modern historical criticism.

The publication of the *Chronicles and Memorials* continued from 1858 to 1911, or fifty-four financial years, during which 253 volumes were issued.[1] Production, however, after reaching totals of 87, 61 and 62 in the three first decades, declined sharply and in the last twenty years only 20 volumes were published. In fact, Maxwell Lyte has recorded that in his day (i.e. from 1886 onwards) only 1 volume, that of Maitland, was commissioned,[2] while after 1898 the only editor to remain in production was L. O. Pike with his series of Year Books. While the origins of the Rolls Series are clear, the immediate and direct causes of its demise are uncertain. Even the official account admits to ignorance on this point. Maxwell Lyte has told us that it was in a decline before he became D.K. 'When I took office,' he said, 'the *Chronicles and Memorials* were, I may say, in very low water.'[3] He had, in fact, stated in his first *Report* that 'the material reduction in the amount allotted for Calendars and Historical Documents has prevented the undertaking of any fresh work during the past year.'[4] In a letter of 1887 he is more specific: 'No fresh work whatever has been undertaken for the series since March 1885,

---

[1] For statistics, see *First Report*, I, pt 2, p. 75. The total number of volumes is there given as 252, with another still to come in 1911. On p. 98a the total is given as 254. On my calculation 250 volumes (excluding those subsequently cancelled) were issued, but three of these were bound in two parts.

[2] *First Report*, I, pt 2, p. 98b, referring to minutes of evidence; ibid., I, pt 3, Q. 545 (p. 21b).

[3] *First Report*, I, pt 3, Q. 539 (p. 21a).

[4] ibid., I, pt 2, p. 98a, and *Deputy Keeper's 48th Report*, p. xvii.

and the successive reductions in the Subhead for Calendars and Historical Documents (the latest being in the current financial year) preclude the idea of undertaking any for the present.' He wrote again in the same year: 'the whole fate of the Rolls Series is precarious.'[1] We can in fact watch the grant diminishing in the annual estimates. By 1891 it had fallen to £1,150 and in 1892 to £750. Thenceforward it did no more than service the outstanding volumes already accepted. What lay behind the decision does not appear. No doubt the lack of enthusiasm on the part of Sir George Jessel, M.R., and his successor W. B. Brett (later Lord Esher) before 1886, and the subsequent desire of Maxwell Lyte to publish record material, were contributory causes, nor must we forget that a heavy building programme was being financed at the Record Office in the early nineties. Nevertheless a suspicion remains that someone, somewhere, in the early eighties or before, had resolved upon the demise of the series.

The printing cost of the normal volume had originally been estimated at £232.[2] This, especially after the original half-leather binding had been replaced by the cloth format stigmatized by Maxwell Lyte as 'abominable,'[3] proved far too generous, and save in exceptional cases the normal cost of a volume of 500 pages was about £110. On the other hand, Romilly had been optimistic in demanding a printing of 1,500, and the more realistic figure of 750 was soon the rule. With initial sales running at about

---

[1] LB, v, p. 270.   [2] LB, i, p. 135.
[3] *First Report*, i, pt 3, QQ. 537–8 (p. 21a); cf. also Q. 797 (p. 61b).

200 plus, there were still copies to spare, and William
Hardy began the distribution of sets to reputable
libraries, with the stipulation, rarely honoured, that
they should be returned if the collection were dis-
persed. Sales, indeed, long remained pitifully low,
but within the present century, with the multiplica-
tion of public libraries and of expert teachers and
research workers in history, a new market has grown
up for the texts, and almost all the useful ones are
out of print.

The volumes, irrespective of size, were sold
originally for 8s 6d, later 10s. The actual cost
of printing varied from 2s 6d to 7s, so that even
after overheads and the commission to Longmans
had been added there was a margin of profit for
direct sales. A semi-official estimate of the costs and
receipts up to 1901 gives the total cost of publication
as £127,000, of which three-fifths (£75,000) went in
editorial fees and two-fifths (£50,000) in printing
and publication.[1] Within the same period the number
of copies sold was 59,046 which, even with allowance
for free copies, was considerably less than half the
number printed. Allowing for the price (8s 6d) in
early years, this would give a gross receipt of some
£28,500. As the Exchequer grant had totalled £67,000
by 1880-1, the funds available, even when the grant
fell to a token in the nineties, would have covered
the editorial costs with a comfortable margin, while
on the sales account the Stationery Office may have
been by 1901 some £25,000 in the red. The total cost
to the nation must therefore have been at that date

[1] See table in *First Report*, 1, pt 2, pp. 85-7.

some £100,000. Subsequent sales will have somewhat reduced this figure.

To the student of the accounts perhaps the greatest surprise comes from the sums paid to the editors.[1] A rough calculation shows Stubbs, with nineteen volumes to his credit, as the highest scorer, with receipts of about £6,600, but H. T. Riley with £6,487 for fifteen volumes, and H. R. Luard with £6,432 for seventeen, run him close. When one allows for the depreciation of the pound since 1914, and the virtual absence of taxation (income tax stood at 6d during most of Stubbs's earning years), these sums would each in purchasing power equal at least £24,000 net of our currency. Such gains must arouse mixed feelings in past and present editors of our Camdens. Moreover, many of the editors had, or allowed themselves to have, a very light task, with only one or two clearly written manuscripts to collate, and no chronological or other problems to unravel in the notes. Lumby with his nine volumes of Higden (beginning at the Creation), Luard with his Matthew Paris, and above all Pike with his fourteen volumes of Year Books, had found steady, unexacting and secure sources of revenue for a long spell of years. No wonder that some of the grossly underpaid clerks at the Record Office took every opportunity to get in on the ground floor, and that subsequent critics have, without justification, regarded the Rolls Series as a scheme of 'jobs for the boys.'

The Rolls Series has come in for a great deal of

[1] These figures are derived from the accounts in P.R.O. 37/18.

adverse criticism ever since the two first volumes were published. It was indeed from the beginning an extraordinarily inexpert affair. It depended in origin and throughout the great productive decades almost entirely upon two men, the one an enlightened and energetic amateur, the other an archivist of great ability with an unrivalled knowledge of the main manuscript resources of the country, but without either a wide knowledge of history or the technical skills of an editor such as were possessed in his day by Georg Waitz, Philipp Jaffé and other disciples of Ranke in Germany, and by Léopold Delisle and others in France. Indeed, the amateur status of many of the editors is only too patent, and it seems well-nigh incredible that they should have had the hardihood to attempt, without any training, to exercise the critical technique which the seminars in Germany and the École des Chartes at Paris were even then bringing to perfection.

Looking back on the enterprise after a hundred years, it would appear that it had from birth two radical faults. Firstly, it was concerned with work wholly outside the statutory province of the Record Office. It was no business of the M.R. and D.K. to supervise editions of works not contained in their own records, and executed by editors who had no connection with the Office or who, if they had, worked out of office hours. Moreover, the Series absorbed funds which might otherwise have gone to record publications, and in the event the final cause of the burial of the Rolls Series was probably the decision of Maxwell Lyte to publish calendars, lists and indexes on the grand scale. Secondly, there was no editorial organization of the kind that had already become necessary to guarantee the selection and scholarly editing of texts, and, once Romilly had gone, there was nobody with authority or interest to give encouragement and coherence to the scheme over a long period of years. The contemporary emergence of history as a foremost academic discipline made it certain that any such undertaking in the future must be directed by trained professional historians, but no attempt was made to bring in scholars such as Stubbs or Maitland in an advisory capacity. The unfortunate relationship of government employer to official employee, which was unconsciously fostered by Romilly and the two Hardys, and gave an unreal and slightly ludicrous tone to some of the correspondence, stood in the way of co-operation, and Maxwell Lyte did nothing to change it. A wider range of experience and counsel would have prevented some of the fiascos and eliminated the unedifying wrangles. Doubtless some of the editors were dilatory and difficult, but co-operative and serial undertakings in our own day have taken a long time to complete without giving rise to quarrels and scandals, and one feels that Sir George Clark, to take an eminent editorial name of today, has known how to ride a horse on the snaffle when a tight rein might have caused accidents.

Nevertheless, when all has been said, the Rolls Series has justified many of the fair hopes of Romilly and Duffus Hardy. Who, among English medievalists of the past seventy years, could have done without it, or would have wished it away? Who will suggest that, had it never come into being, we should even by 1960 have better editions of all the more significant works? And without all these texts it is difficult to see how the great revolution in academic history, which has sprung primarily from medieval constitutional and institutional history, could ever have taken place. That revolution is forever associated with the name of William Stubbs, and it was as editor of the Rolls volumes that Stubbs prepared for himself and for others the tools of the trade.

Problems in Monastic
History

★

The *Regula Magistri*
and the
Rule of St Benedict

Foreword

TWENTY-FIVE years ago few topics in medieval history could have seemed less controversial than the origins of the two documents that marked and moulded two great epochs in monastic history: the *Rule* of St Benedict, and the *Carta Caritatis* of Cîteaux. Today (1962) and now for more than twenty years, an exactly opposite judgment would be valid: no topics in medieval history have been, and are still, more hotly debated. Each has given rise to a voluminous literature; each has attracted the attention of distinguished scholars and inspired a notable group of younger but no less able men; each has led to further research and valuable revisions in neighbouring fields. In each case, also, the spark that started the blaze was struck at a moment when the continent of Europe was about to be shut off by war from England and America, and in a region with which external communications were to cease for five or more years. In this country, therefore, the scholars, relatively few in number, who would have been competent to take part in these controversies, scarcely knew that they existed until they had grown to such proportions as to make it all but impossible to pick up the back-log of the literature, which was scattered over a dozen or more periodicals and *festschriften*, most of which were, and remain, hard enough to come by in England even in times of peace.

In neither controversy has the main issue been

settled decisively, but in each the wind has for the moment ceased to blow at gale force, and the moment seems opportune for presenting medievalists in this country with an account of the points at issue, with a narrative of the various phases of the controversy, and with an assessment of the positive results, which in each case demand an important revision of historical opinion.

Details of the copious literature on this controversy can be extracted from the bibliographical sections of such periodicals as the *Revue d'histoire ecclésiastique*, *Recherches de théologie ancienne et médiévale* and the *Revue Bénédictine*. A chronological and fairly comprehensive list of 113 writings between 1938 and 1957, with other useful information, is given by Dom Odo Zimmermann in his article 'An unsolved problem: the Rule of Saint Benedict and the Rule of the Master,' in the *American Benedictine Review*, x, pts 1–2 (1959), pp. 86–106. Of the surveys by experts the most helpful are those of Christine Mohrmann in *Vigiliae Christianae*, VIII (1954), pp. 239–51, and G. Penco in *Studia Anselmiana*, XXXVIII (1956), pp. 283–306; this is reprinted almost unchanged in the same writer's *S. Benedicti Regula* (Florence 1958), pp. xix–xxxi.

I

The *Regula Magistri*
and the
Rule of St Benedict

(i)

THIRTY years ago, after a generation of scholars including such names as Ludwig Traube, Germain Morin, Ursmer Berlière, André Wilmart, John Chapman and Cuthbert Butler had criticized and extended the work of the Maurists of the eighteenth century, the current account of the *Rule* of St Benedict (henceforward Rule or *RB*) would have run on the following lines. The Rule was the work of a lawgiver of genius who, while taking many hints from the Fathers and early monastic legislators, had produced an eminently original code that reflected its author's personality at every point. We possess this Rule in a text of exceptional purity, carefully copied from a careful copy of the autograph. Though not applied widely at first, the Rule arrived in Rome within thirty or forty years, and was observed at the Lateran monastery, and also at the monastery established on the Coelian Hill by Abbot Gregory, later Pope Gregory the Great, who devoted a whole Book of his *Dialogues* to a life of the saintly founder. Such would have been the general tenor of the common story. It is not too much to say that every statement in the above account has now been challenged, and several, at least, have been disproved.

Before proceeding to give an account of the controversies that have arisen concerning the Rule, it may be well to review the course of criticism in its regard and to record a few motes that have troubled the mind's eye even in the years before the real controversy began.

Manuscripts of the Rule are legion, and it was not till the last decades of the nineteenth century that attempts were made to establish a critical text that might replace the stereotyped version that had held universal sway since the first days of printing. The first editors, Schmidt and Wölflinn,[1] used a restricted number of manuscripts and gave great weight to the oldest known to exist, Oxford Bodleian MS Hatton 48, an Anglo-Saxon text executed probably at Canterbury towards the end of the eighth century. This edition soon came under attack from the great palaeographer Ludwig Traube, a Monumentist. In a treatise[2] which soon became a classic, he traced the history of MS 914 in the library of the ancient abbey of St Gall (Switzerland), and upheld its claim to be a copy by Grimaltus and Tatto, two German monks of the early ninth century, of the codex sent to Charlemagne from Rome in 787, which

---

[1] E. Schmidt, *Regula Sancti Patris Benedicti* (Ratisbon 1880); E. Wölflinn, *Benedicti Regula Monachorum* (Leipzig 1895).

[2] L. Traube, *Textgeschichte der Regula S. Benedicti* (Munich 1898; 2nd ed. by H. Plenkers, 1910).

claimed to be a careful copy of the autograph of
St Benedict himself, long preserved first at Monte
Cassino and then in the papal archive. Traube did
not live to produce a text of the Rule, but he held
that Sangallensis 914, controlled where necessary by
later manuscripts of the same family, was the supreme
authority to be followed, as being for all practical
purposes an autograph. Within a few years Dom
Germain Morin published a superb diplomatic
edition[1] of the St Gall manuscript, but it was
more than ten years before Dom Cuthbert Butler
produced an edition of the Rule which he qualified
as *critico-practica*.[2] In this, he took Sangallensis 914
as his basis, and provided a good working apparatus
of the principal manuscripts, but he aimed at producing a text that might be used in choir and in
chapter and for frequent reading by monks, and
therefore retained some, though not all, of the
classical Latin spelling and grammatical forms that
had currently been substituted for the forms found
in the manuscripts. This compromise did not satisfy
critics and philologists, and in 1928 Dom Benno
Linderbauer of Metten published a text which followed more closely the orthography of the manuscripts.[3] It soon became clear however that the task
of an editor could not be confined simply to replacing
the commonly received text by printing Sangallensis

[1] G. Morin, *Regulae S. Benedicti . . . cod. Sangall.* 914 (Monte Cassino
1900).
[2] E. C. Butler, *S. Benedicti Regula Monasteriorum* (Freiburg-im-
Breisgau 1912; 3rd ed. 1935).
[3] B. Linderbauer, *S. Benedicti Regula Monachorum* (Metten 1922);
S. Benedicti Regula Monasteriorum (Bonn 1928).

914. The oldest extant manuscript, that now at Oxford,[1] and a group of cognates, agreed in showing a number of small additions (together with a few omissions) which were clearly distinct from the linguistic and other changes made in the received text in the interest of clarity and classical Latinity. These variants still remain as an outstanding problem. If, as all modern editors are agreed, Sangallensis 914 is for all practical purposes an autograph, how is it that manuscripts considerably older than the extant witness to the autograph show the presence of another tradition? Are these variants the result of a very early re-editing of the Rule, or do they represent another (presumably earlier) version from the hand of St Benedict himself? In addition to this, many commentators had long felt that some sort of a break occurred in the Rule at the end of chap. 66, and that the final chapters were a later addition made by the saint. There was, in fact, a fairly general agreement on this, though there is no corroborative manuscript authority of any kind. As we shall see, these critical points were to win greater significance in more recent discussions.

In addition, the researches of editors, and in particular those of Butler, into the literary sources of the Rule, had revealed a very considerable amount of borrowing from earlier Rules and directories such as, e.g., Cassian, the Lives of the Fathers and the Rule of St Augustine. Even some of what appeared to be the most personal prescriptions of St Benedict were now seen to be taken directly from older sources.

[1] Bodl. MS Hatton 48.

The number of such direct borrowings, exclusive of
scriptural quotations, was indeed not excessive in
relation to the bulk of the Rule, but it was clear that
St Benedict, like other monastic legislators, took the
best wherever he found it and had no intention of
clothing it with his own words.

As for the saint himself, the testimony of
St Gregory, traditionally so valuable and liturgi-
cally so familiar to monks throughout the centuries,
appeared less helpful to modern eyes. The second
book of the *Dialogues*, which forms part of a survey
of the monastic and eremitical life of contemporary
Italy, is concentrated almost entirely upon signs
and wonders and is of little help as a study of the
life and character and achievement of St Benedict.
There is only one explicit reference in the *Dialogues*
to the Rule,[1] and apart from this the Rule has no
literary mention in the abundant source material of
the period until *circa* 630.[2] St Benedict himself has
no mention before 680. Monte Cassino was destroyed
by the Lombards in 570, and though it may be
accepted that the community fled to Rome and was
lodged at the Lateran, there is no certain evidence
of its permanence there.

In other words, the modern monk or critic,
searching for the historical portrait of the patriarch
of Western monasticism, found the darkness falling
the nearer he approached the lifetime of St Benedict,
and was left finally with the Rule as the only clear

[1] *Liber Dialogorum*, II, 36.
[2] In the letter of Abbot Venerandus of Altaripa to Bishop Constantius
of Albi, printed by Traube, *Textgeschichte*, p. 87.

monument, supported as it was by the wise remark of Gregory that the writer of such a Rule could not but have been a living example of its spirit. Nevertheless, the Rule was there, a genuine acorn from which the Benedictine centuries had sprung. Indeed, in 1929 Abbot Chapman[1] had endeavoured to exhibit St Benedict as a celebrated miracle-worker, commissioned by a pope, probably Hormisdas, to write a basic Rule for the West, phrases of which were even caught up into the legislation of Justinian. Few accepted the characteristically brilliant if somewhat irresponsible hypothesis, and subsequent scholars, with few exceptions, have ceased to consider it as tenable, but the long-term result of the book in all its parts was to emphasize the traditional picture of a majestic and wise father-figure, celebrated all over Italy of his day and writing his Rule for an unspecified but wide body of monks.

Such was the state of opinion in the 1930s. A generation of distinguished scholars was beginning to disappear, and early monastic history was in the doldrums and had given place to medieval monasticism in the interest of most Benedictine scholars. Then, in 1937, a small cloud appeared on the horizon. Dom Augustin Génestout, a monk of Solesmes, had been for some years in residence at Sant' Anselmo in Rome as Procurator in Curia of the Congregation of France. He occupied his leisure in making preparations for an edition of the Rule. In 1937 the abbots of the whole Benedictine world congregated in Rome for one of their periodical reunions, and

[1] H. J. Chapman, *St Benedict and the Sixth Century* (London 1929).

when they returned home they brought news that
Dom Génestout was talking about an opinion that
he was going to put forward, to the effect that much
of the Rule of St Benedict was borrowed directly
from a document known as the Rule of the Master,
of which very few Benedictines had ever heard.
Silence followed for a year. Then, in the latter part
of 1938, Dom Alamó of Silos blew the gaff in a
short article in the *Revue d'histoire ecclésiastique*.[1]
Another monk of Silos, Dom Pérez de Urbel, had
been studying the *Regula Magistri* without controversial intent; he accepted without question the
current assumption that the Master had pillaged
the *RB*, and went on to argue that this anonymous
Rule was the work of a Spanish monk in the early
seventh century.[2] Dom Alamó, who had had relations
with Dom Génestout and was eager to refute his
Spanish confrère, jumped the gun with a *non placet*
in which he used some of the arguments he had
heard to show that the Master's dates were earlier
than those of St Benedict, and that the saint had
taken from him some important parts of the Rule.
His arguments were brief, but telling: the voca-
bularies of the two writers were different; the disciplinary practices of the two Rules differed; and the
liturgical framework showed striking divergencies. In
every case the Master seemed clearly to represent an
older tradition than St Benedict. Dom Pérez, who
had seen this article before publication, wrote a short

---

[1] 'La Règle de S. Benoît éclairée par sa source, la Règle du Maître,'
in *R.H.E.*, xxxiv (1938), pp. 739-55.
[2] 'La Règle du Maître,' ibid., pp. 707-39.

rejoinder in the same number of the *Revue*, in which he scouted the novel theory.[1] Nevertheless, the heather had been set alight and fire-fighters and fire-raisers alike hastened to the spot. There was, as was natural, a strong conservative reaction among the established Benedictine scholars. Abbot Capelle and Dom Lambot of Mont-César (Louvain), Abbot Herwegen of Maria-Laach, Dom Philibert Schmitz of Maredsous, editor of the *Revue Bénédictine*, and Dom Justin McCann, a monk of Ampleforth and Master of St Benet's Hall at Oxford, were united in demonstrating the inferiority of the Master's Rule *vis-à-vis* that of St Benedict, and in arguing that it would be a moral and literary impossibility for a religious genius to have drawn inspiration from such a polluted source. At this point the fall of France occurred, and the controversy was silenced so far as English readers were concerned.

Henceforth, for several years, two circumstances combined to bedevil the discussion. One, that could not have been foreseen or avoided, was the advent of war, which prevented scholars outside continental Europe from keeping *au courant* and made the exchange of ideas and literature difficult even within the territories controlled by Germany. The other circumstance, which might well have been averted, was the confusion caused by the thesis of Dom Génestout having been touched off at half-cock before its author was in a position to display all his arguments in print. As a consequence of this,

---

[1] 'Le Maître et S. Benoît,' ibid., pp. 756–64.

several years elapsed before his opponents had a clear view of the target: the conservatives began to defend *RB* before Génestout had deployed his attack, while on the other hand his first exposition, when it came, took no notice of the objections that had been made already to some of his arguments. But before proceeding to a narrative of the conflict, it is necessary to glance at the document that caused all the trouble, and to ask ourselves, as did many Benedictines at the time, 'What is the *Regula Magistri?*' (*RM*).

(ii)

The *RM* is no discovery of modern scholarship. It had circulated in the monastic world since the days of Louis the Pious. The title given to it in the earliest manuscripts is *Regula Sanctorum Patrum*, on account of four short directories, bearing the names of four fathers of early monachism, which precede the longer anonymous composition with which we have to deal. The title which has stuck to it for more than a thousand years was bestowed by St Benedict of Aniane in his *Concordia Regularum* drawn up early in the ninth century.[1] He had a reason for the name: the normal opening of a chapter in the work is the formula: 'The question of the disciple. The Lord answered through the Master.' The piece was first printed, along with the other rules in Benedict's collection, by Holstenius

---

[1] *Codex Regularum*, ed. L. Holstenius (Rome 1661), II, pp. 293–462.

in Rome in 1661, and was subsequently reprinted
from the edition of 1759 by Migne in vol. 88 of his
Patrologia Latina.[1] Subsequently it had been used
by editors and commentators of *RB* to illustrate
monastic practice. There was therefore no secret
about it, or of the fact that many of the topics and
a considerable proportion of the actual text of *RB*
was to be found in it, but there had been unanimity
among scholars in assuming or accepting that the
author of *RM* had pillaged *RB*. In default of any
indication of date in *RM*, and of any attempt to go
behind the *Concordia Regularum* to criticize the
manuscripts, this assumption was very natural. *RM*
is a long and often rambling document, three times
as long as *RB*, in which deep spiritual wisdom
jostles picturesque narrative and queer practice.[2]
The prologue and first ten chapters of *RM* are
almost identical with the prologue and first seven
chapters of *RB*; after that the parallels and resemblances are frequent, though irregular and less striking, down to chap. 66 of *RB*, which corresponds
to the last chapter of *RM*; a phrase or two of a later
chapter of *RB* resembles passages in an earlier
chapter of *RM*. It was natural that those who had
been brought up to know *RB* by heart, and to
regard it as a unique spiritual guide, should assume
that the borrowing had been done by the writer

---

[1] Migne, *P.L.*, vol. 88, cols. 943–1052.

[2] Early in the controversy the traditionalists used extravagant language about *RM*, and even Penco writes of it 'come una farragine
ampollosa di prescrizioni bizarre, raccolte in un dettato di incredibile
prolissità' (*S. Benedicti Regula*, p. xxi). In fact, the greater part of *RM*
is sober and reasonable, with many wise injunctions.

who was clearly the less gifted and less spiritually mature of the two. Granted this, a detailed examination of RM would have seemed a mere waste of time, and in fact no scholar had attempted it.

In consequence, as has been noted, the first reaction to the novel theory was on the whole hostile. Benedictine scholars took down their volume of Migne and read RM for the first time, only to be amused, bored or exasperated by turns. It seemed unthinkable that such a compilation, lacking all sense of proportion, naïve at times and even distasteful, could be a primary source of some of the most familiar and hallowed chapters of RB, while it seemed entirely plausible that the author of such a rag-bag should have lifted useful sections from RB. Some writers, as for example Dom Justin McCann, the only Englishman to be 'in on' the controversy before the war, made of this their chief argument and cited at length the seemingly ridiculous passages of RM.[1] Even Abbot Ildefons Herwegen, a critical historian of eminence, could write as late as 1944 that Génestout's view 'ist als absurd zurückzuweisen.'[2]

The first scholar to come to grips with the Master in the conservative interest was Dom Bernard Capelle, abbot of Mont-César, Louvain.[3] By training a critic

[1] 'The Rule of the Master,' in *Downside Review*, LVII (1939), pp. 3–22; 'The Master's Rule again,' ibid., LVIII (1940), pp. 150–9.

[2] L. Herwegen, *Sinn und Geist der Benediktinerregel* (Einsiedeln 1944), p. 396, n.1; Dom G. Morin also held to the traditional view in 1944 in *La Règle de S. Benoît* (Fribourg), p. 12.

[3] 'Cassien, le Maître, et S, Benoît,' in *R.T.A.M.*, XI (1939), pp. 110–18.

of texts, he found a 'control' in Cassian, and compared the quotations from him that were common to
RM and *RB*, concluding that while some passages
seemed to show the priority of *RB*, the three most
conclusive passages agreed in showing that the Master
followed his model more closely than did St Benedict,
and that therefore *RB* in these passages was following *RM*. This, however, was not what Capelle was
out to prove; he therefore put forward the suggestion,
destined to find fortune in the sequel, that while *RB*
in the text known to us depended at least in places
on *RM*, the latter depended in turn upon an earlier
recension of *RB*. Whether Capelle realized it at the
time or not, this was a clever tactical move, since it
enabled the supporters of *RB* to have it either way;
if *RM* agreed with *RB* there was no difficulty, the
Master was following Benedict; if, however, *RM*
seemed nearer to any particular control than *RB*,
then the Master was following an early version of
RB, specifically, one stopping at chap. 66, a version
which many critics had posited as a necessary
explanation of the terminal phrase of that chapter.
Almost simultaneously, Dom Justin McCann defended the conservative view in the *Downside Review*,[1]
and a few months later Capelle reiterated his opinions
in a second article. Meanwhile the still silent Génestout had found a champion in the distinguished
Jesuit patristic scholar and editor of the *Revue
d'Ascétique et de Mystique*, Père F. Cavallera, who,
untroubled by any feelings of family piety, contributed to his periodical a linguistic examination of

[1] See above, n. 15.

RM and expressed his entire agreement with the
conclusions of Dom Alamó.[1] He followed this up
in the same year by a second article defending the
spiritual teaching of the Master.[2]

At last, early in 1940, the long-awaited exposition
by Dom Génestout appeared.[3] The writer explained
that his article had been written a year previously
after three years' intensive study of the matter. It
was therefore an exposition, not a polemic. His thesis
was that *RM* was composed early in the fifth century
in Dacia by or under the influence of Bishop Nicetas
of Remesiana, but he did not elaborate this suggestion
and it may be said at once that this authorship has
been eliminated and this locality strongly criticized
in subsequent discussion,[4] though the early date for
the nucleus of *RM* found some favour with scholars.
Génestout's arguments for the priority and early date
of *RM* were many; the monastic practices there
described were clearly more primitive than those of
RB; there was no hierarchy of officials, and no mention of ceremonies at profession. Liturgical practice
was likewise more primitive: there were no hymns
in *RM* and no cursus of psalms appropriated to particular hours. Several passages were examined, particularly in the Prologues of the two works, and in the

[1] 'Aux origines de la Règle de S. Benoît,' in *R.T.A.M.*, XI (1939),
pp. 375–88.

[2] 'La *Regula Magistri* et la Règle de S. Benoît,' in *R.A.M.*, XX (1939),
pp. 225–36; 'La *Regula Magistri*: sa doctrine spirituelle,' pp. 337–68.

[3] 'La Règle du Maître et la Règle de saint Benoît,' in *R.A.M.*, XXI
(1940), pp. 51–112.

[4] e.g., by J. Zeiller of the Sorbonne in 'Un ancien évêque d'Illyricum
peut-être auteur du *Te Deum*: Saint Nicéta de Remesiana,' in *Académie
des Inscriptions et Belles-Lettres, Comptes rendus* (1942), pp. 356–69, and
J. Leclercq in *Rev Bén*, LVII (1947), pp. 210–12.

chapter (the second in *RB*) on the abbot, where the
longer text of *RB* in certain passages seemed expli-
cable only as containing sentences interpolated by the
later writer, i.e. St Benedict. Moreover, *RM* gave
every sign of integrity as a whole, which of itself
was proof of anterior composition. The manuscripts
of *RM* were analysed, and dated as *c.* 600 and
c. 650–700, but this, Génestout submitted, did not
prove that the original composition was later than
that of *RB*. Dom Génestout also sought to prove
that a set of verses, prefacing the Rule in some
manuscripts and critically edited by Traube, contained a clear statement of the Master's achievement;
this conclusion was arrived at by lowering a capital
in the word *Simplicius* and giving a capital to *magistri*
in the line following. Here again, it may be said at
once that subsequent criticism has eliminated this
suggestion, by which Génestout had hoped to clinch
his thesis.[1]

The appearance of this article was almost coincident with the fall of France, which effectively
isolated the controversy within the territories occupied by the victorious German armies. Capelle
replied to Génestout almost at once,[2] confining
himself to textual arguments; he challenged some
of the passages alleged by Génestout, and explained
the most important by recourse to his own theory
of the two recensions of *RB*. Meanwhile Dom Pérez

---

[1] See B. Capelle, 'Un plaidoyer pour la Règle du Maître,' in *R.T.A.M.*,
XII (1940), pp. 5–32; A. Lambert (of Ligugé), 'Autour de la Règle du
Maître,' in *Revue Mabillon*, XXXII (1942), pp. 21–79.

[2] See preceding note.

de Urbel, in an omnibus reply to Alamo, Cavallera and Génestout, reiterated his theory of a Spanish origin, and of John of Biclaro (d. 621) as author.[1] His conclusions have not won wide support, and his dating has been decisively rejected, but some of his arguments from monastic practices and liturgy have force, and he did well to assert that the controversy was too wide in its implications to be settled by the comparison of a few texts, where ingenious arguments might be made to tell either way.

Génestout's article, as it gradually percolated through war-riven Europe, initiated what may be called the 'free-for-all' epoch of the debate, when combatants fought single combats or fired lonely guns into the void. The year 1944–5 marked the entrance of two new critics, both of whom were to show staying-power. The one was Dom Hubert Vanderhoven of St André, Belgium, who was to help in giving the *Regula Magistri* a firm textual basis, though his first essay was of no great significance[2]; the other, Dom Robert Weber of Clervaux, Luxembourg, came forward in support of the traditional priority of *RB*, though he was compelled to adopt Capelle's theory of the two recensions in order to explain anomalies.[3]

The year 1946 was relatively quiet, though Vanderhoven made an interesting liturgical point

---

[1] 'El Maestro, San Benito, y Juan Biclarense,' in *Hispania*, I (1940), pp. 7–42; II (1941), pp. 3–52.

[2] 'S. Benoît a-t-il connu la règle du Maître?' in *R.H.E.*, XL (1944–5), pp. 176–87.

[3] 'Interpolation ou omission? A propos de le règle de S. Benoît et de celle du Maître,' in *Revue des études latines*, XXIII (1946), pp. 119–34.

when he saw in the puzzling phrase of *RB*, (xvii, 2) 'Singillatim et non sub una Gloria,' a direct rejection of a strange practice, to which *RM* referred, of allowing brethren pressed for time to recite token verses of the psalms followed by a Gloria,[1] while Dom Jacques Froger of Solesmes, in a monograph on the origins of the office of Prime, fixed on *c.* 500 as the date of its introduction into the Office, thus giving a *terminus a quo* for *RM*.[2] There followed two important articles by Dom Génestout, which did not, however, fully accomplish his promise to treat the whole matter *in extenso*. In the first[3] he accumulated more arguments bearing upon the date of the principal manuscript of *RM* and of *RM* itself; in the other,[4] by means of a lengthy examination of the scriptural quotations of the two Rules, he carried the matter a distinct step forward: *RM*, despite its apparently disparate character, was shown to have a unity of its own in matters of style and treatment; Vanderhoven followed to show that certain passages in *RM*, and among them one or two of those most frequently held up to ridicule, were certainly or very probably interpolations.[5] He was supported by Dr François Masai, Keeper and later Librarian of

---

[1] ' "Singillatim et non sub una Gloria." Qu'a voulu dire S. Benoît?' in *Revue du moyen âge latin*, II (1946), pp. 301–8.

[2] J. Froger, *Les Origines du Prime* (Rome 1946).

[3] 'Le plus ancien témoin manuscrit de la Règle du Maître: le Parisinus latin 12634,' in *Scriptorium*, I (1946–7), pp. 129–42.

[4] 'Unité de composition de la règle de S. Benoît et de la règle du Maître d'après leur manière d'introduire les citations de l'Écriture,' in *St.Ans.*, XVIII–XIX (1947), pp. 227–72.

[5] 'Les plus anciens manuscrits de la règle du Maître transmettent un texte interpolé,' in *Scriptorium*, I (1946–7), pp. 193–212.

Manuscripts at the Royal Library of Brussels.[1] Masai
was the first layman, and save for Cavallera, the first
scholar outside the monastic order to enter the lists.

The general result of all this was to show that
RM, whatever the date of its existing manuscripts,
was in fact a text of some age and standing by the
end of the sixth century, and that further intensive
study in this direction was a *sine qua non* of further
progress. This, however, did not deter scholars in
different parts of Europe who had by now mastered
the materials from putting forward various views.
Thus Dom F. Renner of St Ottilien, working on
Capelle's theory of a twofold *RB*, endeavoured to
reconstruct the development from *RB i* through
RM to *RB ii*.[2] Some years later, he followed this
up by another long study,[3] in which he argued that
RM was composed in southern Italy between 535
and 546, depending upon *RB i*, and completed before the publication, some time after 546, of *RB ii*.
Capelle had therefore two able disciples in Weber
and Renner, and the theory of the double *RB* was
kept well in the foreground of the controversy. Meanwhile, Génestout, in a fourth article (his last)[4] provided a vigorous and on the whole persuasive defence
of *RM* as a spiritual document and monastic code; he
showed that the practices that had been described as

---

[1] 'La règle de saint Benoît et la *Regula Magistri*,' in *Latomus*, VI (1947),
pp. 207–29.

[2] 'Textschichten und Entstehungsphasen der Benediktinerregel. Die
Magisterregel in Kreuzverhör,' in *Benediktus*, XXVII (1947), pp. 397–474.

[3] 'Die Genesis der Benediktus- und Magisterregel,' in *S.M.*, LXII
(1950), pp. 87–195.

[4] 'La Règle du Maître n'était-elle pas digne d'être utilisée par
S. Benoît,' in *S.M.*, LXI (1947–8), pp. 77–92.

strange or coarse were current in monastic circles of the age.

Others by now were seeking for an author for *RM*, and Dom Cappuyns, of Mont César, found him in the great Cassiodorus. According to Cappuyns,[1] who followed his abbot's opinion of the twofold *RB*, Cassiodorus wrote *RM* with the earlier version of *RB* before him. Masai refuted Cappuyns's arguments for Cassiodoran authorship on linguistic grounds, though admitting the connection with his monastery, Vivarium.[2] Two more adherents of the Capelle theory next came forward: Professor Ezio Franceschini, of the Milan Catholic University,[3] and Dom François Vandenbroucke of Mont César, who used the statistical method of the Cambridge mathematician Yule in an endeavour to show that both the Rules were composite (i.e. that the vocabulary indicated that neither was the work of a single writer) and that the matter common to the two rules was earlier in date than that of either (the second) *RB* or the rest of *RM*.[4] Dom Vanderhoven criticized the findings of both these scholars.[5] Masai meanwhile had been doing some careful linguistic research, and on one apparently small point he

[1] 'L'auteur de la *Regula Magistri*: Cassiodore,' in *R.T.A.M.*, xv (1948), pp. 209–68.

[2] 'Cassiodore peut-il être l'auteur de la *Regula Magistri?*' in *Scriptorium* II (1948), pp. 292–6.

[3] 'La polemica sull'originalità della regola di S. Benedetto,' in *Aevum* XXIII (1949), pp. 52–72.

[4] 'Saint Benoît, le Maître et Cassiodore. Faits nouveaux,' in *R.T.A.M.* XVI (1949), pp. 186–226.

[5] 'Règle du Maître, statistiques et manuscrits,' in *Scriptorium*, III (1949), pp. 246–54.

registered a significant discovery.[1] Taking the common introductory word *autem* he found that whereas in the portions of *RB* peculiar to Benedict *autem* is used eighty-one times, *RM* uses the word only eight times in its whole length, not including direct quotations from Scripture. Meanwhile Vandenbroucke had followed up his somewhat unsatisfactory statistical article by one of the most valuable contributions in the whole literature of the controversy,[2] in which he discussed in the first place the literary sources and the date of composition of *RM* and *RB*, having in each case subtracted the sections verbally common to both, and then applied the same test to this third common section, which he labelled *S* (= source). He was able to establish the irreducible literary characteristics of the two Rules and to show that *S* showed solidarity with *RM* and not with *RB*. The source-material behind all three documents showed the same differences and resemblances, and Vandenbroucke dated section *S* as post-536. As for *RM*, this was dated 555–75, but this late date was solely due to his admission of Cassiodorus as a source—an inclusion which few scholars were willing to concede. Cassiodorus apart, the date for *RM* would be somewhat earlier than that for *RB*, say 520.

There followed, in quick succession, three articles

[1] 'Observations sur la langue de saint Benoît et du Maître,' in *Miscellanea J. Gessler*, II (1948), pp. 845–54. For a discussion, see *Settimane di Studio del centro Italiano di Studi sull' alto Medioevo IV* (1957), pp. 444–5.

[2] 'Sur les sources de la règle bénédictine et de la *Regula Magistri*,' in *Rev.Bén.*, LXII (1952), pp. 216–73.

proposing novel theories. Dom Louis Brou of Quarr Abbey, while editing some liturgical prayers, declared that *RM* was in fact the first version of *RB*, and that the present *RB* came into being in Gaul early in the seventh century.[1] We shall see later how research on the text of *RB* soon entered into the stream of the *RM* controversy. Next Dom Odo Zimmerman, monk of Tepeyac, Mexico City, improving upon Brou's thesis, maintained that *RM* and *RB* were both the work of St Benedict, being earlier and later versions of his Rule.[2] Finally, a new arrival, Dom Pierre Blanchard of Solesmes, put forward a novel version of the traditional view. *RM* had its origin at Bobbio in the early seventh century, and was based on *RB*.[3] This theory was speedily exploded on chronological grounds,[4] when the earliest-known manuscript of *RM*, itself far from the archetype, was shown to have been written *c.* 600, that is, before the foundation of Bobbio (613).

[1] *The Psalter Collects*, Henry Bradshaw Society, LXXXIII (London 1949). Brou was following suggestions of Froget in this.

[2] 'The *Regula Magistri*: the Primitive Rule of St Benedict,' in *American Benedictine Review*, I (1950), pp. 11–36.

[3] 'La Règle du Maître et la règle de saint Benoît,' in *Rev.Bén.*, LX (1950), pp. 25–64.

[4] H. Vanderhoven, 'La règle du Maître et la règle de saint Benoît,' in *R.H.E.*, XLV (1950), pp. 707–10.

(iii)

By this time it had become clear that no further decisive work could be attempted until the manuscripts of *RM* had been critically edited and firmly dated. It was known that Dom Vanderhoven and Dr. François Masai had undertaken the task, and it was accomplished in a remarkably short space of time when the very complicated typographical problems are taken into account; its appearance in 1953 marks the beginning of a new epoch in the history of the controversy.[1] Before carrying the story further it may be well to review the manuscript tradition of *RM*.

The text of the Master's Rule is preserved in three manuscripts only: Paris B.N. lat. 12205; Munich lat. 28118; and a Cologne manuscript which is a late copy of the Munich one. In addition there are five manuscripts of extracts, including one of early date (Paris B.N. lat. 12634) giving a purer text than the complete Paris manuscript. The Munich manuscript is a ninth-century text of the *Concordia Regularum* of Benedict of Aniane from which the old printed edition of *RM* derives. In these circumstances the editors decided that a critical edition would be an impossibility and therefore provided a diplomatic edition of the two Paris manuscripts, with the readings of the Munich

---

[1] *Aux sources du monachisme bénédictine. I: La Règle du Maître.* Publications de Scriptorium, III (Brussels/Paris 1953).

manuscript in the apparatus of Paris 12205. The
book that resulted was universally acclaimed as a
masterpiece of careful editing and exquisite typography. Every detail of the original manuscript is
represented by a device of printing. To the criticism
that a photographic reproduction would have been
no more expensive, the editors replied that passages
in the manuscripts could only be read with great
difficulty and by means of artificial aid, and would
have been unreadable in a photograph. Critics also
drew attention to the extreme complexity of the *sigla*,
which does indeed make a careful reading a very
laborious performance, in which the context and even
the sense of a clause is often forgotten, but the
editors had certainly succeeded in making the text
of *RM* available to scholars in a form that gave all
necessary information for critical and textual arguments. The volume also contained diplomatic, palaeographical and linguistic dissertations: the last of these,
by Mr P. B. Corbett,[1] did not escape criticism. The
judgments of the editors on the probable origins,
antiquity, authorship and literary history of *RM*
were reserved for a second volume. This, after
eight years, has not yet appeared, but as the three
scholars concerned have written or spoken elsewhere
on the whole matter it would not seem that any
surprise is in store for us. All three have made it
clear that they regard *RB* rather than *RM* as
derivative.

The *Scriptorium* volume injected new life into a

---

[1] At that time Mr Corbett was a lecturer in the Department of
Humanity at Aberdeen University.

controversy that had shown signs of flagging through lack of new material. In the first place it provided a reliable text of the two principal manuscripts for all who could buy or obtain access to the volume (725 frs. belg. = £5 7s); philological and textual points could now be firmly based, no longer relying on the treacherous text of Migne. Next, it gave final confirmation to what had come to be generally accepted, viz., that no extant manuscript of *RM* antedated the composition of *RB*. The editors dated 12634 as 580–600, and 12205 as 600; E. A. Lowe reverses the two dates.[1] The great problem therefore cannot be resolved by palaeography. Thirdly, it showed, at least to the satisfaction of the editors, that the two crucial Paris manuscripts represented different stages in what may be assumed to be a long development of *RM*. Fourthly, the editors, as palaeographers, assigned a south Italian (and possibly a Vivarium) provenance to both manuscripts. This, of course, as the editors themselves point out, is no firm evidence of Campanian origin for *RM* itself.

Meanwhile, at almost the same moment as the publication of the edition of *RM*, two other controversies blew up which were not in origin connected with it, but which helped to clear the air and improve visibility. The first arose from a very long and crabbed article by Dom P. Paringer[2] of

---

[1] Masai dates 12634 as late sixth cent., and 12205 *c.* 600 (*La Règle du Maître*, pp. 59–60). Lowe (*Codices Latini Antiquiores*, v (Oxford 1950)), nos. 623 and 646, dates 12634 as 600+ and 12205 as −600.

[2] 'Le manuscrit de Saint-Gall 914 represente-t-il le latin original de la Règle de saint Benoît?' in *Rev.Bén.*, LXI (1951), pp. 81–140.

Wettenburg, in which he endeavoured to show that Sangallensis 914, so far from being only two removes from the autograph of St Benedict, and therefore to be accepted as the primary authority for the text of *RB*, was (according to him) a barbarous text and probably the work of Anglo-Saxon copyists. Paringer did not survive the publication of his article for many months, and was therefore spared the pain of seeing its demise. A few critics gave it a favourable reception, but scholars were saved expense of time upon it in the following year, when it was shot down with a single barrel by the eminent late-Latin philologist, Professor Christine Mohrmann of Nijmegen University, who had no difficulty in showing that the St Gall manuscript was written precisely in the grammatical and orthographical style of central Italy in the sixth century. This article,[1] and a further study written for a new printing of Dom Philibert Schmitz's edition of the *RB*,[2] have been of permanent value both to students of *RB* and in subsequent discussions of the respective dates of *RB* and *RM*.

Meanwhile, Paringer's attack on Traube may be regarded as an incident in the movement that led to and is still moulding a considerable and fruitful re-examination of the manuscript tradition of *RB*, and a series of editions has appeared in quick succession which may or may not have attained to finality, but which have driven, not only Butler, but Linderbauer also, off the market. Schmitz, Steidle, Lentini, Penco

[1] 'La latinité de S. Benoît,' in *Rev.Bén.*, LXII (1952), pp. 108–39.
[2] *Sancti Benedicti Regula* (2nd ed., Maredsous 1955).

and Hanslik[1] have all produced texts, of which that
of Schmitz is notable for the introductory treatise on
the Latin of St Benedict of which mention has
already been made, that of Steidle for its rich introductory matter, that of Lentini for its division of
each chapter into 'verses' which will probably become
stereotyped in all future editions, and that of Penco
for its valuable introductory matter, for the admission
of *RM* into the critical apparatus and for an elaborate
commentary which, together with the other elements,
forms the fullest examination hitherto given of the
liturgical and disciplinary background of monastic
life in the early sixth century. As for Hanslik's edition,
it at least fulfils the promise given some sixty years
ago when H. Plenkers undertook to prepare a text
for the Vienna *Corpus Scriptorum Ecclesiasticorum
Latinorum*. Plenkers had originally outlined for himself a wide programme which included an edition of
several other monastic Rules, and had been overtaken
by the First World War long before he mastered the
Herculean labours of collating and classifying the
innumerable manuscripts contained or concealed in
the libraries of Europe. Though he was unwilling to
relinquish his task, he fell down at last upon his
assignment after thirty years, and the long-awaited
volume has now appeared in a form very different
from that of fifty years ago, and in a climate of
scholarship that neither Plenkers nor Butler would
have recognized. The appearance of Hanslik's text

[1] B. Steidle, *Die Regel St Benedikts* (Beuron 1952); A. Lentini,
S. Benedetto, La Regola (Monte Cassino 1947); G. Penco, *Sancti Benedicti
Regula* (Florence 1958); R. Hanslik, *Benedicti Regula* (Corpus Scriptorum
Ecclesiasticorum Latinorum, LXXV (Vienna 1960)).

is too recent for one who is not an expert to anti-
cipate the final verdict of textual scholars, but two
features are immediately apparent: the apparatus and
appendices are of unusual richness and will serve as
tools for future scholars; while on the other hand the
editor, as a logical consequence of his judgment upon
the *RM*, admits readings from its manuscripts only
as valuable indications of an early tradition of the
text, and that only in passages where the verbal
resemblance is almost complete. He gives no indication of the many passages where the resemblances
between *RM* and *RB* are clear, but only partial, and
the reader is therefore unable to use Hanslik's text
as a control for his own examination of the two
Rules.

The bomb dropped by Paringer was still occupy-
ing the attention of the disposal-squad when another
arrived, threatening still wider devastation. This had
been prepared by Dom Jacques Froger, who was no
stranger to the field. He now came forward with the
suggestion that *RM* and *RB* represented two stages
in the evolution of a single document.[1] The Master
was no other than Benedict himself, and *RM* was
Benedict's original Rule. This of itself would have
resembled Brou's or Capelle's theory, but Froger,
realizing that the difference between the two Rules
was too great for any suggestion of common authorship, even after the lapse of twenty years, had the
hardihood to suggest that *RB* never appeared in the
sixth century, and that *RM* was reduced to a work-

[1] 'La Règle du Maître et les sources du monachisme bénédictin,' in
R.A.M., xxx (1954), pp. 275–88.

able code early in the seventh century by, or through
the agency of, the Gallic abbot Venerandus, who, it
will be remembered, was associated with the first
clear mention (with a single distinguished exception)
of the Rule of St Benedict. The exception was
St Gregory the Great, with his celebrated phrase
which all Benedictines know (or should know) by
heart, but Dom Froger was prepared to stick at
nothing, and asserted as it were in passing and
almost as a point on which there could scarcely be
two opinions, that St Gregory's words referred to
RM, which they suited admirably. This was the most
revolutionary of all the suggestions made in the controversy; if true, it would have deprived the historical
Benedict of Monte Cassino of his unique title to fame
and veneration, and would have transformed the
effective authorship of *RB* to an unknown Gallic
abbot or monk. For a short time cautious scholars
refrained from using the designation 'Rule of
St Benedict' for *RB* and substituted that of the
'*Rule obsculta*,' while a few, acting on the principle
that a committed critic must always load the dice
in favour of his opponents, accepted the disappearance
of their patron as a regrettable necessity. It was not
long, however, before the forces of tradition rallied.
Athwart the passage of Froger's theory, whatever he
might say or omit to say, stood the text of St Gregory,
in which the pope had remarked that Benedict of
Monte Cassino had written a Rule *discretione perspicua
et sermone luculenta*, and had proceeded to infer that
the writer of such a Rule must have resembled in
character the wisdom of the work. Discretion and

clarity (*lux*) were not the characteristics that had appeared to be the most significant notes of *RM*, nor were most Benedictine scholars as yet willing to admit that St Gregory himself showed no further influence from *RB*. In the event, Dom Froger received his final quietus from two quarters: the first was an increasing familiarity with the findings of Miss Mohrmann, that the language of *RB* was characteristic of the mid-sixth century, and the second a long examination[1] of St Gregory's writings by Dom Anskario Mundó, in which that scholar assembled indications of every kind to show that *RB* dated from *c.* 530–50, and showed moreover that a passage in St Gregory's *Dialogues* recorded an observance in the Rule followed at Monte Cassino which was in agreement with *RB* but contradicted *RM*; the passage, moreover, carried a clear verbal echo of *RB*.[2] The Benedictine authorship of *RB* may therefore be accepted more confidently (if possible) than ever.

The appearance of the *Scriptorium* edition of the *RM*, together with the critical disquisitions accompanying it, had the effect of muting the controversy in its original form. It was accepted by almost all those familiar with the literature to date that the priority of *RM* as a monastic document had been established as a working hypothesis of extreme probability, but that no absolutely compelling evidence could be brought to prove this on purely textual or

---

[1] 'L'authenticité de la Regula Sancti Benedicti,' in *St.Ans.*, XLII (1957), pp. 105–58. See also the Spoleto discussion (above, n. 42), pp. 453–5.

[2] St Gregory, *Libri Dialogorum*, II, 12; cf. *S. Benedicti Regula*, chap. li.

palaeographical grounds. Pending, therefore, the discovery of totally new material, it was the task of all
interested scholars to examine with care the whole
field of early sixth-century monastic discipline and
liturgical practice, and at the same time to pursue,
with regard to *RM* in particular, the philological
examination outlined by Christine Mohrmann.

Consequently, the last eight years or so have seen
the publication of numerous articles and studies
directed towards these ends, and the great controversy in its latest phase has been of service in
polarizing the interests and sharpening the wits of
a new generation of monastic scholars whose talents
might otherwise have been devoted to topics of lesser
actuality. Among these Dom Anscario Mundó of
Montserrat and the younger Dom Gregorio Penco
of Finalpia have been pre-eminent. The latter in
particular has displayed extraordinary energy in following up his doctoral thesis on the subject with a
baker's dozen of studies,[1] all based on careful critical
work, particularly in the field of liturgy, which has
served as material to be digested and reproduced in
the introduction and commentary to his edition of
RB. The general result of all these has been to
strengthen the impression both of the logical and
chronological posteriority of *RB* and of its direct
dependence upon *RM*. The appearance of the long-
awaited edition of *RB* in the Vienna Corpus came
therefore as something of a shock and a disappointment, for both in Dr Hanslik's introduction and
apparatus and in the critical dissertation that appeared

[1] They are listed in Penco's edition of the Rule, p. xv.

almost simultaneously from his pupil, Miss Theresia Payr,[1] the priority of *RB* was flatly asserted, by Hanslik *tout court* and by Miss Payr with the rider that a common document might lie behind both Rules.[2] The reader therefore who wishes for a full discussion of the relationship of the *RB* to *RM* must have recourse to the edition by Dom Penco, which preceded Hanslik's by a year, and which gives full readings of the two Paris manuscripts of *RM* and indicates all parallel, as well as all identical, passages.

(iv)

At the end of this long and perhaps tedious review, where do we stand? Let us first consider the present state of our knowledge of the two documents, and then proceed to examine their mutual relationships. We will begin with *RB*.

RB, as a text, has issued from the mêlée relatively unscathed. Traube's exposition of the unique fidelity of Sangallensis 914 has been impugned, but not exploded. There is a general agreement that that manuscript is an accurate, but not a photographically exact, reflection of the text of *RB* as it passed from its author's hands at the end (it may be) of a complicated process of composition. The language and

---

[1] 'Der Magistertext in der Überlieferungsgeschichte der Benediktiner-regel,' in *St.Ans.*, XLIV (1959), pp. 1–84.

[2] Miss Payr suggests (art. cit., p. 83) that, faced with the differences and similarities of the two Rules, 'meinen wir auch Annahme einer gemeinsamen Quelle für die Regula Magistri und die Regula Benedicti erklären zu können.'

orthography are those of the mid-sixth century, and
could not possibly have been devised by a writer or
scribe of the ninth or even of the seventh century.
There is also general agreement that the first recension of *RB* originally ended with chap. 66, and that
the remaining seven chapters (some would say six
of the seven, the last of all being part of the original
version)[1] were added later. But it should be empha-
sized that no trace of, or reference to, the shorter
version has been found, and the significance of the
first recension in relation to the *RM* remains one of
the unsolved problems of the controversy. The
circumstance that an early version of *RB* ends
where *RM* ends also, though at first sight arresting,
cannot be made to guide us as to the relative priority
of either. There are, however, traces of another early
version, usually known as the 'interpolated' text,
although it is remarkable for omissions also as well
as for additional matter. This has no connection
with the two recensions already mentioned, and
Hanslik[2] would see in it the work of a Roman
abbot or monk of the seventh century, acting in the
interests of clarity or simplicity. Few would now feel
satisfied that the Italian archetype of Sangallensis 914
was the actual autograph of St Benedict, and it has
recently been demonstrated by Hanslik[3] that the
existing manuscript is only a copy of the copy of the
Aachen manuscript which was taken by Grimaltus and
Tatto, but when all has been said, the St Gall

---

[1] So, e.g., Penco, *Regula*, p. 280.

[2] *S. Benedicti Regula*, chap. li.

[3] ibid., chaps. xxvi–xxix. See also the Spoleto discussion (above, n. 1,
p. 157), pp. 448ff.

manuscript derives from the original text by a very short series of copies done by unusually careful scribes, and scarcely any other work of the early Middle Ages can show such a pure descent. If to Hanslik's apparatus and concordance we add the critical commentary of Penco and the display of the sources in the last (1935) edition of the Butler Rule, it will be seen that *RB* can enter the critical lists in almost perfect fighting trim.

The same cannot be said of *RM*. The *Scriptorium* diplomatic edition is indeed an extremely elaborate and accurate piece of work, and provides all the evidence available for its text, but the documents themselves are accidental survivals of two different streams of manuscript tradition and give clear indication of internal rearrangements and long interpolations. With only a single complete text available a critical edition in the ordinary sense is impossible, and we have no reason to suppose that the Paris manuscripts are particularly faithful witnesses, or that they show evidence of direct kinship to the manuscript of *RM* which (according to one hypothesis) was used by St Benedict. Moreover, we have as yet no concordance to these texts, and their contents are generally unfamiliar, whereas many know *RB* almost by heart. As regards the date of these manuscripts all are now agreed that both can be assigned to a space of time within ten or twenty years on one side or the other of A.D. 600, but there is a fair measure of agreement that they show signs of internal rearrangement and considerable interpolation which implies an already lengthy manuscript tradition and makes it impossible to be sure of the state of the text half a century or more before they were written, when the hypothetic connection between *RM* and *RB* took place. Finally, no fully adequate work has been done on the language of *RM*, though there is agreement that both the Paris manuscripts have a south-Italian provenance, possibly from Vivarium.

As to the date, provenance and identity of the Master we have the following suggestions:

1 Perez de Urbel. Spain, *c.* 600. *John of Biclaro.*
2 Génestout. Dacia, fifth century. *Circle of Nicetas of Remesiana.*
3 Alamó. Near Rome, early fifth century. Gomez, ditto, 525–60.
4 Cappuyns. Vivarium, *c.* 555. *Cassiodorus.*
5 Zimmermann and Froger. Monte Cassino, *c.* 530. *St Benedict.*
6 Blanchard. Bobbio, *c.* 600.
7 Renner. S. Italy, 535–46.
8 Masai. S. France, *c.* 490–500. (The original nucleus.)
9 Penco. Lérins, 530–540.

It is fairly easy to eliminate several of these theories. The date of the manuscripts of *RM* eliminate John of Biclaro; the early sixth-century date of composition, accepted now almost universally, invalidates Génestout's guess. Zimmermann and Froger, and their whole thesis, are exploded by the certainty that *RB* existed *c.* 545. Blanchard's

opinion is ruled out by the date of foundation of
Bobbio and the date of the manuscripts. Cappuyns
has failed to convince most scholars that *RM* could
by any possibility have been written by Cassiodorus.
We are left with a group who agree on a date round
about 500–20 for the bulk of *RM*, but disagree in
suggesting S. Italy, near Rome, and S. France as the
region. The one apparent clue to locality in *RM*, the
reference to some vagrant monks as coming 'a finibus
Italiae,' has proved, as have so many arguments in
this controversy, a double-edged weapon. The phrase
has been taken as meaning either 'from the Italian
land' as opposed to 'from near at hand,' or 'from the
ends of Italy.' Both phrases would be compatible
with a south-Gallic provenance and the second would
be compatible with a situation either towards the
north or towards the south of Italy. The latest trend
is to look for the author in S. Gaul near the Pyrenees,
but neither Lérins nor Marseilles can be wholly ruled
out.

The ultimate problem we are considering has
often been put in the simple form of an alternative.
Of the two texts *RM* and *RB* one must be copied
from the other; it is our task to discover which is
the original. As will by now have become clear, this
is an undue simplification of the problem, for other
solutions have been proposed; but it is at least the
basic dilemma put in its simplest form, which must
be faced sooner or later by the investigator.

The first attempts to solve the problem made use
of the discipline obvious in all cases when two pieces
of writing are compared, viz., that of textual criti-

cism. Which text, according to the approved rules of this technique, now several centuries old, is the original and which the copy? Unfortunately, after more than twenty years, and despite the efforts and assertions of numerous well-qualified scholars, the verdict of an outsider must be: *non liquet*. Though this line of argument was used with great effect by the early advocates of *RM*, the latest workers in the field, Dr Hanslik and his pupil Miss Payr, are equally resolute in defending the priority of *RB* on purely textual evidence. Though an observer who is uncommitted may feel convinced by the arguments of this party or that, it is clear that, as things stand now, a decisive argument must be sought elsewhere. Probably these particular texts are not patient of tests of the normal editorial kind, which have to deal with the work of numerous scribes engaged on copying a single text. In the matter we are concerned with, the two authors, the Master and St Benedict, are engaged *ex hypothesi* not on copying, but on adapting a text which is itself often little short of a *cento* of passages from older documents. Nor can we be quite certain that either of the texts we are using is precisely that used by each author when the act of transcription took place, for our text of *RM* is at least fifty years later, and that of *RB* may not be exactly what was available to the Master, if it were he who followed St Benedict. Consequently, in any particular passage some cause other than that of the normal psychophysical reaction of a scribe may have been at work. Unfortunately, several of those who have attempted to solve the question by proofs of a textual kind have been content to use a small number of examples, and tacitly to adopt the position that a single clear instance of priority in one or other of the documents proves the case. But in a matter like this, as in the comparable case of the problems of New Testament text-history, the chain is not in fact as weak as its weakest link—or, to put the matter more correctly, a single minute point, in which various circumstances and personal judgments *could* have played their part, is not in fact a vital link. It may be true that a scribe naturally tends to adopt or to provide the *lectio facilior*, but he is a free agent, and when he is also a mature and original writer, it is always possible that some motive of which we have no knowledge may have influenced his choice of words. Moreover, the possibility of mutual reaction cannot be excluded. For myself, after reading all the articles in which textual criticism has been employed, I feel that those who seek to demonstrate the dependence of *RB* upon *RM* win heavily on points, but that there are undoubtedly several passages in which, when they are considered in isolation, the textual dependence may well seem to be the other way round, and in consequence no way exists, within this particular technique, of resolving or eliminating these obdurate contradictions. As we have seen, these difficulties drove some scholars to posit the existence of a double recension of *RB* in order to explain the apparent two-way influence of the documents. Unfortunately, the textual critic *de métier*, trained exclusively in the methods used for centuries in establishing and castigating classical and scriptural texts, is often blind to the limitations of his technique. It was disappointing, at this time of day, to find Dr Hanslik resting his case for the priority of *RB* on a handful of passages and the assertion that, as a textual critic, he could only abide by the proof they gave. When it is a question of basic authenticity and authorship the textual critic must take account of arguments of wider ambience than his own.

This apparent clash of evidence caused scholars, even in the early days of this controversy, to abandon the arguments of verbal textual criticism for those of vocabulary, language and arrangement. Here a method was to hand which seemed likely to give valuable results. In whatever way the interdependence is expressed, all agree that there are long passages virtually common to *RB* and *RM*. These have been listed and in several cases examined thoroughly by Renner and Vanderhoven, though unfortunately the references they give are to the Migne edition of *RM*. They comprise primarily the Prologue and chaps. 1–7 of *RB*, and may conveniently be denoted by the *siglum* BM (= Benedict-Master). Now it is clear that if we reshuffle our two documents into *RM-BM* (= M) and *RB-BM* (= B) and *BM*, we can compare the language and usages of *BM* with each of its two constituents and note not only the major differences between *BM* and *RB*, but also those between each and *BM*, thus possibly discovering which of the two partners is preponderant in the sections common to both. We can also go on to examine the literary sources peculiar to each of the three divisions and thus perhaps arrive at a decision as to their respective dates. Of all the purely internal tests this would seem to be the most promising, and it has in fact provided fairly clear conclusions when applied by several scholars.

The first to use it was Génestout, who passed in review all the scriptural citations in the two documents, noting the frequency of various terms and phrases. In all such exercises the personal element of choice and interpretation must play a part, and some of Génestout's figures have been questioned, but his general conclusion appears valid, that *BM* throughout shows solidarity with *M* and differs sharply from *B*. Thus the word *scriptura* is used more than forty times in *M* to introduce a quotation, whereas there is not a single instance in *B*, where the word only occurs twice, in both cases in quite different context. Similarly, *M* uses parts of the verb *dicere* some two hundred times when introducing a quotation, whereas *B* has the verb in this way only six times. Within a year of Génestout's article, Masai, using the same method in another field, arrived at the same conclusions. Taking the common conjunction *autem*, he found it, as we have seen, extremely common in *B* (eighty times), but rare and, if scriptural quotations are excluded, almost non-existent in *M + BM* (eight times). Other observations made by Masai and Penco all point in the same direction; thus *magister* and its derivatives appear nowhere in *B* but frequently in *BM* and *M*. *Schola*, a word familiar to all monks from the familiar phrase in the Prologue—*constituenda est ergo a nobis dominici schola servitii*—is never found in *B* (the quotation is of course in *BM*) but is common in *M*. Similarly, *discipulus*, common in *M* and *BM*, is found once only in *B*; *monachus*, on the other hand, is common in *B* but rare in *M*. Similarly, whereas *B* prefers *Deus* to *Dominus* in the ratio of forty-four to thirteen, *M* prefers *Dominus* to *Deus* in the ratio of forty-five to five. Equally striking observations can be made of single words. Thus in the chapter on obedience which occurs in *BM* a scriptural quotation occurs, introduced by the words: *Et item dicit doctoribus*.[1] Probably few, even among Benedictines, would be able to answer without hesitation if asked who these doctors were. The reference is in fact to Luke 10:16, where the 'doctors' are the seventy-two disciples, but the word occurs nowhere else in *BM* or *B*, but is familiar in *M*, where the significance of the term is explained.

The cumulative weight of these and similar examples of verbal usage is very great. Unlike the purely textual arguments it reflects the author's settled and subconscious bent of mind, not the isolated idiosyncrasy or mechanical reaction of a copyist. It is indeed possible to bring arguments against this or that instance, but the number of words and phrases that have been adduced is large and the reiterated force of the proof is great. No traditionalist has succeeded or even attempted to adduce contrary evidence, and the conclusion would seem to be clear: that *RM* and *RB* have an entirely different verbal usage the one from the other, and

---

[1] *S. Benedicti Regula*, chap. v.

that in the passages common to both *RM* shows itself as by far the most influential partner. The conclusion that *RB* is following *RM* would therefore seem to impose itself beyond question.

One of the happier results of the controversy has been to set scholars to work over the whole field of monastic life and institutions in the early sixth century, and much has been written in recent years of the differences between *RM* and *RB* in matters of liturgy and monastic observance. It is generally acknowledged that the liturgical usages of *RM* are more archaic than those of *RB*, and that the latter has a clearer and more integrated scheme. This would not necessarily prove the priority of *RM*, for in the general flux of the age a district or a monastery might well remain in a backwater; the traditionalists are right in emphasizing the wide range of contemporary practice from S. Italy to Spain. Nevertheless, if we consider some of the differences we may be able to draw some conclusions.

It would, in the first place, be quite impossible to extract a daily horarium from *RM*, or to define the alterations of observance in the various seasons, whereas in *RB* the main lines of the day and the year stand out clearly, however much we may regret the absence of clock time or the lack of a calendar of saints' days. A few examples may be given. While *RM* has a long period of graded fasting, beginning immediately after Epiphany and reaching a physical climax in Holy Week, *RB* has a clear-cut season, beginning on the sixth Sunday before Easter, with an undifferentiated fast, and Lent is regarded in *RB*

not only as a time of fasting, but as one of private
mortification and spiritual renewal. Whether or no
the legislator was of set purpose following the Roman
custom may not be clear, but the liberal use made of
the Lenten discourse of Leo the Great cannot be
without significance. Of greater importance for our
purpose are the strictly liturgical regulations. In *RM*
there is no *cursus psalmorum*, no assignment of psalms
to particular offices, but a steady passage through the
psalter. This contrasts strongly with the precise and
often purposeful arrangement of *RB*, in which the
shorter psalms are reserved for the minor hours and
vespers, and certain psalms, such as those at compline
and that said before the invitatory at mattins, are
chosen because of their intrinsic suitability. In addition, *RM* makes use of a group of canticles instead
of psalms at lauds, whereas *RB* has only a single
canticle each day, thus following, as is explicitly
stated, the usage of the Roman Church. Among the
parts of the office that *RB* rendered standard monastic
practice are the *Kyrie eleison* (ordered by the Council
of Orange, 529), the *Te Deum*, the initial *Deus in
adjutorium* and the *Ambrosiana* or hymns. None of
these is in *RM*, whereas the latter has the archaic
practice of inserting collects between psalms and uses
responsorial psalmody. Indeed, the liturgical evidence
of greater antiquity in *RM* is overwhelming, and
although this does not necessarily or even probably
imply priority in date of composition or use, it is
hard to believe that the compiler of such a liturgical
directory could have seen and appropriated a
great part of a Rule such as *RB*, where clarity

and order reign with such evidence, without
modifying his own liturgical practice at least in
some respects.

If we examine the sources used in the three
sections *RM*, *BM* and *RB*, the same differences are
apparent as in the use of words and phrases. While
RM has a distinct penchant for the apocryphal Acts
and Passions of the apostles and martyrs that circulated in the fifth and early sixth centuries, such as
the *Visio Pauli*, the *Acts* of St Silvester and the
Passions of SS Eugenia, Sebastian and Anastasia,
the only two quotations from such sources in our Rule
are two in chap. 7, which is common to *RM* and *RB*.
The treatment of Cassian is particularly significant.
He is quoted frequently by both *RM* and *RB*, and
occurs repeatedly in *BM*, but there is a general
agreement, such as is rare in this controversy, particularly on a textual point, that the quotations in *BM*
are derived from *RM*, which is consistently nearer to
the text of Cassian than is *RB*. Indeed, this solidarity of *BM* and *RM* in the matter of Cassian has
formed one of the strongest technical arguments for
the priority of *RM* since its use at the very beginning
of the controversy by Alamó and Génestout, and it
was this admitted dependence that drove Capelle and
later Weber to the hypothesis of a double redaction
of *RB*, the second version having been contaminated
by *RM*.

In this source-material, perhaps the most controversial name is that of Cassiodorus, which, like
that of Cassian, has given rise not only to a difference
of opinion, but to a new hypothesis. Cassiodorus is

never cited by *RB*, *et pour cause*, since his spiritual
writings date from after *c*. 545. If therefore *RM* cites
him this would place the document well and truly
posterior to *RB*. Cappuyns, it will be remembered,
had gone so far as to put forward Cassiodorus as the
author of *RB*, though such a view must be regarded
as untenable. Vandenbroucke, while not following
Cappuyns thus far, nevertheless was ready to accept
some borrowing from Cassiodorus by *RM* and
accordingly put the earliest date for its composition
c. 555–75. The arguments for a literary dependence
of *RM* upon Cassiodorus are, however, far from
strong, and can be reduced to a single plausible
instance. Even this, which turns upon a sequence
of scriptural quotations, occurs in a passage loaded
with verses from the Bible, and could be explained
equally well, if necessary, as a borrowing in the
reverse direction by Cassiodorus.[1] This must make
us hesitant in accepting it as proof positive, all the
more because this single instance of borrowing, if
proved, would compel us to accept once and for all
the priority of *RB* over *RM*. Rather than place a
load on a base so fragile, it is perhaps wiser to leave
this argument out of the reckoning.

If we now consider the field of monastic discipline
and observance we shall find here also wide difference
between the Master and St Benedict. The most striking is perhaps the monolithic nature of authority in
RM. Modern and even late-medieval fashions of
thought have led commentators to regard the abbot

[1] See the article by Vandenbroucke, 'Sur les sources etc. (above, n. 43),
and Penco, *Regula*, chaps. xxvii, xlv–xlvii.

of *RB* as possessed of tremendous if not excessive power, but he appears as a limited, if not constitutional, monarch when compared with the sovereign of the *RM*. In this the abbot is an autocrat; there is no chapter as in *RB* on the twofold source of counsel for the abbot—that of the whole community and that of the seniors—and in the *RM* the abbot appoints his deans and his successor without taking advice. Very significantly, where *RB* has the chapter-title *De ordine congregationis*, *RM* has *De honore vel gradum* [*sic*] *post abbatem ceteris denegandum*,[1] and it proceeds to give a series of directions imposing a rigidly egalitarian regime upon the brethren. This stands in direct contrast not only to the hierarchy of officials in *RB*, but also to the instructions scattered through the *RB* which imply mutual reverence and obedience between old and young, and the right of the former to something of a privileged position, while the democratic election of the abbot in *RB* and the nomination of a prior with right of succession by the dying abbot of *RM* are clear indications of opposing outlooks. It is true that St Benedict, in what is almost the only clear expression of personal opinion in *RB*, gives utterance to his dislike of a second-in-command, and animadverts on the nuisance a prior can be,[2] but he nevertheless bows to the ruling opinion in favour of a prior, and the very phrase he uses of troublesome lieutenants—that they think themselves to be second abbots—would seem to be a glance

---

[1] *RB*, chap. lxiii; *RM*, chap. xcii.

[2] *RB*, chap. lxv; *RM*, chap. xciii. 'Dum sint aliqui maligno spiritu superbiae inflati, et aestimantes se secundos esse abbates' etc.

at the prior with right of succession as described in *RM*.[1]

Finally, the rite of profession in *RB*, which takes place at the end of the year of probation, is at once a simple and a comprehensive ceremony, whereas in *RM* the various elements, such as renunciation of ownership, promise of stability, reception of a new habit, are spread out across the year, and it is difficult to say when the decisive promise is made.

These examples do not exhaust the list of points in which *RB* differs from *RM*. All show the genius of the author of *RB* for providing a combination of simplicity and completeness which is absent from the diffuse and yet often incomplete scheme of *RM*. It is very difficult to suppose in this field also, that any reasonably intelligent legislator would have failed to accept some, at least, of these sane, simple and practical directions.

[1] cf. the remarkable phrase in *RM*, ed. Vanderhoven (above, n. 1, p. 159), p. 313: 'Nam istum [sc. the prior with right of succession] per actum bonae observantiae vel [sc. et] nimia humilitate et Deus elegit et abbas consensit et sacerdos ordinavit . . . unde ex illa die quasi jam spiritalis Caesar designatus secus abbatem sedeat,' etc. This should be set beside *RB*, chap. lxv: 'in illis locis ubi ab eodem sacerdote vel [sc. et] ab eis abbatibus qui abbatem ordinant, ab ipsis etiam et praepositus ordinatur . . . aestimantes se secundos esse abbates, adsumentes sibi tyrranidem.' This passage surely is proof that St Benedict was familiar with *RM* and the customs there described; it shows also that the author of this passage of *RM* was familiar with the practice in the later Roman Empire of the Emperor (*Augustus*) designating his coadjutor with right of succession (*Caesar*).

(v)

After this long exposition, how may we best present the various opinions that have been put forward? They may be reduced to five groups:

I There is, first, the traditional opinion that *RB* is prior to *RM*, which (if the modern word be allowed) is in large measure a plagiarization. This has been held by Perez de Urbel, McCann, Lambert, Frank, Lentini, Toribros Ramos, Franceschini, Blanchard and Heiming, and in gross, it would seem, by the most recent editor of *RB*, Hanslik.

II Next, there is the original theory of Génestout, that *RM* precedes *RB tout court*. This view has found relatively few supporters among the scholars who have expressed their view in print, but those few are a very powerful group. Besides Alamó and Cavallera, it includes Vanderhoven, Masai, Gindele and Penco, while from outside Dom Jean Leclercq is in agreement.

III Thirdly, there is the theory of mutual dependence, according to which the first recension of *RB* was followed by *RM*, which in its turn influenced to a small degree the second recension of *RB*. One version of this view postulates a (wholly hypothetical) early version of *RB* which has disappeared; another version makes use of a later recension of *RB* which has been thought, quite apart from the *RM* controversy, to lie behind the so-called 'interpolated' text of *RB*. This theory, in one form or another, has rallied a numerous and competent, if somewhat curiously assorted, group of scholars, including Capelle, Weber, Renner, Cappuyns, Vandenbroucke (at least in early days) and Heiming. It may be described as a compromise theory, since it originated in attempts to account for the opposing difficulties that perplex the supporters of both the clear-cut opinions.

IV There is the suggestion that both *RM* and *RB* depend upon a hypothetic earlier document that lies behind the general plan and the material common to both *RM* and *RB*. This would seem to be the opinion of Miss Payr, and it has found favour with others.

All these opinions have operated within, or nearly within, the area covered by existing documents, taking into account their data and their difficulties. In addition, there have been several brave attempts to solve the problem as it were by force. Though different in detail, they may be considered as a single group.

V (*a*) Brou threw out the suggestion in 1949 that *RM* was in fact the primitive *RB*, while the current *RB* was a seventh-century Gallic summary.

    (*b*) Zimmermann in 1950 would have it that *RM* and *RB* were both the work of St Benedict though separated in time by a considerable span of years.

    (*c*) Froger, in 1954, developing the position of Brou, held that *RM* was the work of

13

St Benedict, while *RB* was written up by
Abbot Venerandus in Gaul in the early mid-
seventh century. Gomez, in 1956, held a
similar view.

We may pass judgment on these different opinions
in reverse order.

The various forms of the view that would make
Benedict of Monte Cassino the author of *RM*,
whether as a first draft of *RB* or as his only work,
would seem to be wholly indefensible. Attractive as
the former of the two suggestions might seem at
first, as answering so satisfactorily all the difficult
problems of interdependence, and possibly accep-
table as it might be in the matter of dating, the
proved literary and what may be called 'doctrinal'
and 'liturgical' differences are so great and so well
defined as to preclude any theory of single authorship even over a period of twenty years. As for the
suggestion of Brou and Froger, the existence of *RB*,
as we know it, in the middle of the sixth century has
been proved by every argument save the physical
evidence of a codex of the required date attributed
to St Benedict, or of a reference to the Rule by an
exact contemporary. Conversely, all attempts to
assign *RB* to a date later than the lifetime of St Benedict have failed.

We are left, then, with three possibilities: that *RM*
was used by Benedict; that *RB* was used by the
Master; and that both Benedict and the Master used
an existing document lying behind *BM*. The third of
these views, recently sponsored by Payr and Hanslik,

is superficially attractive as a bolt-hole for the irresolute. It removes all awkward problems into never-
never land. Looked at more critically, however, it
would appear to be untenable. In the first place it
posits as the solvent of all problems an entirely hypothetical document. Beyond that, no-one has said or
can ever say what that document should contain. The
block of material common to both RM and RB, which
we have denoted BM, would, if isolated from all else,
be meaningless, a mere fragment of a Rule. Moreover, there are numerous phrases and passages in the
remainder of RM which were clearly known to the
author of RB (or, conversely, phrases in RB which
were familiar to the Master), and if these and their
context are added to BM we are beginning to get
something very like either RM or RB. If on the other
hand we take it as granted that RM is in general
copying RB, and that our lost document is merely a
short collection of passages in regard to which there
is universal agreement that RM appears to be the
original authority (a Q), we are then in the presence
of one of those ingenious hypotheses, familiar to all
editors of critical texts, which are watertight on paper,
but so subtle and refined as to be morally impossible
to use in practice.

We are therefore thrown back upon the original
dilemma between RB and RM as model, between the
traditionalists and the critics, between Génestout and
Lentini or McCann. In this predicament our choice,
though it may go against the grain to make it, is surely
clear. The traditionalists have no strong arguments
save their ingrained belief in the originality of

St Benedict. Their strongest suit is the textual
argument, in a few passages where *RB* seems, at
least at first sight, to have been the model for *RM*.
The traditionalists have indeed destroyed some arguments of the critics and have countered some which
they have not destroyed, and the critics have in many
details cancelled each other out, but so far as I am
aware no conservative scholar has ever faced and
fought the solid and cumulative force of all the critical arguments as deployed in the past few years, and
as set out in the foregoing pages. No attempt has been
made to refute the case that has been made out for
the priority of *RM* by means of arguments from
language, ways of expression, chronology, liturgy,
monastic discipline and the rest. The critics, for
their part, have all the big guns at their disposal and
have showed themselves as well off for small arms as
their opponents, while they have also been in a position to make use of many of the most powerful arguments of some of their opponents, such as Vandenbroucke and Renner, while not agreeing with their
final conclusion. Indeed, Masai and Vanderhoven on
the one hand and Penco on the other have put up
such a barrage, especially in the years between 1954
and 1959, that they have to all appearances silenced
the older generation of traditionalists. That Hanslik
and Payr could revive the conservative thesis was due
almost entirely to their concentration, to the exclusion
of all else, upon purely textual points, and within that
field upon a very narrow sector.

No-one, it would seem, of the many combatants,
has withdrawn from the in-fighting to contemplate

the battlefield from above. Granted the priority of *RM*, it is possible to see how St Benedict, with the genius that he shows elsewhere in his Rule, may have selected what seemed to him to be valuable, but it is very hard to see by what mental process the Master, who shows himself to have had a very clear conception of the life of a monastery, should have borrowed so much from *RB* and woven it so tightly into his longer code, picking the thread up in the middle of his long Introduction or Prologue, and carefully omitting in that Prologue what to all subsequent ages have seemed the most characteristic and wise of St Benedict's utterances.

If, finally, it is asked what effect the recognition of the priority of *RM* over *RB* will have on our estimate of the legislator of Monte Cassino, three observations must suffice. The first is, that *RB* as we have it may still without any hesitation be considered as the directory compiled by the abbot of the Mount, the last word of a great legislator, the document which ultimately made its way and conquered the monastic world by its intrinsic excellence, and by that alone. In other words, the code of Benedictine monachism stands where it always stood. Secondly, it must be admitted that the abbot of Monte Cassino loses some part of his claim to a unique position among monastic spiritual writers. Not only the greater part of the Prologue, which has been learnt by heart by so many generations of monks for more than a millennium, and the chapter on humility, which has been the subject of so much careful, not to say laboured, comment by monks and theologians from

St Thomas Aquinas downwards, and the chapter on the abbot, which is certainly a masterpiece of spiritual wisdom, but many other passages must now be credited to a nameless predecessor of our patriarch. St Benedict as a master of the spiritual direction of a monastery must now take a more truly historical place as an eminent member of a series or group of sixth-century legislators, rather than an isolated summit of original attainment.

Nevertheless, our third observation must be that the manner in which St Benedict makes use of *RM* and succeeds by small but effective alterations in producing a code which is quite different, not only in arrangement but in spirit and in practicability, is very remarkable. The particular type of monastery, and the particular type of spiritual doctrine which have been considered in the past as characteristically Benedictine, will remain so. The moderation, the humanity, the supple, articulated and yet tightly knit ordering of all the parts and activities of a monastery, the liturgical genius which was to impose its creation on the whole of Western monachism, and by reflection on the whole of the Western church, the streamlined constitution, so comprehensive and yet so adaptable, all these are Benedict's, and his alone. The conviction of so many centuries, that the Rule of St Benedict has a characteristic, easily recognizable 'spirit,' was and is a valid conviction. Statistics may show a grammatical and linguistic difference between the parts of *RB* which are taken from *RM* and those from the remainder of the Rule, but it will be found very often that even in the parts which are in the main common to both documents the phrase or the precept that has stuck in the memory is the work of the writer of *RB* alone. If the dependence of *RB* upon *RM* is accepted, the celebrated description of *RB* by St Gregory the Great is not less, but more, accurate than when this dependence was still unsuspected. One might almost think that the pope knew what St Benedict had done with his exemplar when he spoke of the rule which was *discretione perspicua, sermone luculenta*.

I have sometimes been asked, and perhaps some of my readers will have wondered, why this controversy should have shown itself so perplexed and so interminable. Two reasons, among many, have contributed greatly towards creating this perplexity of counsel. The first, and more superficial, may be found in accidental circumstances. The controversy, as we have seen, began, as it were, before the state of the question was clearly known, and when the stage of sporadic probing had not yet passed the learned world was disorganized by World War II. In consequence, it was several years before the essential points of the case were isolated and expounded and recognized; meanwhile, a great deal of energy was misdirected, and much laborious work tended to litter rather than to clean up the arena. Added to this, contributions to the controversy were scattered among some thirty periodicals and collections in six different languages, and few students can have been able to obtain access to all. I myself have failed to reach two or three pieces, after exhausting the resources of the University Libraries of Cambridge and London, of the Bodleian, of the British Museum and of private monastic sources, and this great physical difficulty has had the result that few of those who have taken part have had a complete knowledge of all that has already been said or suggested or settled, and they have consequently flogged dead horses, passed red lights, pushed at open doors and barked up the wrong tree. Sometimes even, through a sense of frustration, they have abandoned any hope of contributing to an understanding of the matter. If every writer had been able and willing to find out exactly how things stood before he wrote, the literature of the controversy would have been less bulky, but perhaps more helpful, and some at least of the hazardous guesses would never have reached the printed page.

Yet if all this accidental confusion could have been avoided the basic difficulty would have remained. The focus of the whole dispute is a document (*RM*) which is anonymous, of uncertain provenance and date, composite and interpolated, and represented (for all practical purposes) by a single complete manuscript which was written certainly several decades and probably almost a century later than the original from which it descends. As if this were not enough the whole question turns upon the relationship of this great unknown with another document (*RB*) whose exact date is uncertain, which is itself composite and possibly only one survival of two or three versions, and of which we have no manuscript that is physically near-contemporary. It is true, as we have seen, that arguments of various kinds can establish probabilities which to some or to most minds may seem moral certainties, but they are arguments of a kind that can be rebutted or ignored with a fair show of plausibility, or at least without clear absurdity. They are not apodictic; and unless or until a manuscript of the Master's Rule, or a clear proof of authorship, is forthcoming to establish at least an approximate date, it will be possible for ingenious or irresponsible scholars to challenge any conclusion that may be propounded.

Finally, as all who have weighed in on the controversy will allow, and as the abundant literature with its arguments backwards and forwards shows, the documents are peculiarly impatient of any clearcut solution. It might have been hoped that when two texts run side by side for long distances, with additions and omissions now on this side and now on that, it would be easy to see who is copying what, the more so since all agree that the basic style and outlook of the Master and St Benedict are clearly distinguishable. Yet a lengthy study of these passages, such as the Prologue, the chapter on the abbot and the chapters on humility and the instruments of good works, is a frustrating experience. There is no clear answer or argument, and although I myself feel reasonably sure that it is Benedict who is inserting some passages and omitting others in the document before him, I am only too conscious that there are indications that tell the other way, and it is in the end easier, in the purely literary field, to see the objections to each alternative than to accept the positive reasons in favour of either as the original. I can think of no other text where the same frustrating hesitations occur save in that crux of Franciscan studies, the *Legend of the Three Companions*, where something of the same situation occurs—two or more non-literary writers using a common store of earlier material. It is no doubt this confusing pattern of the text that has driven so many scholars to adopt the hypothesis of a two-way influence from one to the other and back again. Certainly this would give the most facile explanation of the recalcitrant facts; it would allow us, for example, to see *RB* as the original text behind much of the chapter on the abbot, whereas *RM* may be allowed to have priority with the Prologue. But to adopt this hypothesis—for it can never be more than that—is in effect to renounce all hope of a demonstrable solution to our problem.

Such, then, is the state of affairs, and for a moment there is something of a lull. Short of some happy discovery of a new manuscript or clear literary evidence, what can be done to hasten a solution of the problem? There would seem to be two main directions for research. The one leads towards a fuller knowledge of the literature, codes and institutions of sixth-century monachism. The more we know of the language and manners of the world in which—somewhere, somewhen—the Master lived and wrote, the more likely are we to be able to discover his exact date and habitat. The second field of research is the detailed linguistic examination of *RM*. A concordance to *RB* already exists in Hanslik's edition. If we had such a tool at our disposal for *RM* we should have a precious yardstick for use in our comparison of the two documents, and in the process of defining the characteristics and differences.

Let our last word, therefore, be this. In our present state of knowledge, the case for the priority of the Master seems stronger by far than the case for the priority of St Benedict as defended by the conservatives. The thesis of the Master's priority may never be proved to demonstration, but it is hard to see that its opponents can ever regain the ground that they have lost in the past twenty-five years, and, unless some wholly unforeseeable discovery is made, the hypothesis that St Benedict made extensive use of the previously existing Rule of the Master must remain as one enjoying a very high degree of probability.

The Primitive Cistercian
Documents

The following is a list of articles by J-A. Lefèvre bearing on the early Cistercian documents. Few research students can have achieved such fame before defending their thesis.

In *Collectanea ordinis Cisterciensium Reformatorum*
'La véritable Carta Caritatis primitive et son évolution (1114–19),' XVI (1954), pp. 5–29.
'La véritable constitution cistercienne de 1119,' ibid., pp. 77–104.
'A propos de la composition de Instituta Generalis Capituli apud Cistercium,' ibid., pp. 157–82.
'Pour une nouvelle datation de Instituta Generalis Capituli apud Cistercium,' ibid., pp. 241–66.
'Les traditions manuscrites des Usus Conversorum de Cîteaux au xiie siècle,' XVII (1955), pp. 11–38.
'L'évolution des Usus Conversorum de Cîteaux,' ibid., pp. 65–97.
'Un texte inconnu de l'Exordium Cistercii et de la Summa Cartae Caritatis dans le MS Melun 55,' ibid., pp. 265–71.

In *Le Moyen Age*
'Le vrai récit primitif des origines de Cîteaux est-il l'Exordium Parvum?' LXI (1955), pp. 79–120; continued ibid., pp. 329–61.

In *Revue Bénédictine*
'A propos d'une nouveau texte de la Carta Caritatis Prior dans le MS Metz 1247,' LXV (1955), pp. 90–112.

In *Cistercienser Chronik*
'Une bulle inconnue d'Alexandre III dans le MS Dijon 87,' LXII (1955), pp. 1–8.

In *Revue d'histoire ecclésiastique*
'Que savons-nous du Cîteaux primitif?' LI (1956), pp. 5–41.

In *Analecta Bollandiana*
'S. Robert de Molesme,' LXXIV (1956), pp. 50–63.

2

The Primitive Cistercian Documents

SOME eighty years ago, the then librarian of the municipal library of Dijon published from among its manuscripts a collection which he entitled *Les monuments primitifs de la Règle Cistercienne*,[1] containing the essential descriptive and legislative documents of the Cistercian order. The abbey of Cîteaux lay only a few miles to the south of Dijon, and when the general dispersal of the libraries of the religious orders took place after the French Revolution, the library of the town received a large portion of the abbey's archives and collection of manuscripts. In the book with which we are concerned, Guignard included the Rule of St Benedict in Latin and Old French, a liturgical directory and a calendar, but the documents which interest us are the *Exordium Cisterciensis Cenobii*, the *Carta Caritatis* and the *Instituta Capituli Generalis*. The *Exordium* is an account of the foundation of the abbey, the *Carta Caritatis* is the document which established the constitution of the Cistercian order, and the *Instituta* are the disciplinary decrees made from time to time by the

---

[1] Ed. Guignard (Dijon 1878), from MSS 601 (*Carta*), 633 (*Exordium*) and 114 (*Instituta*). These documents have since been re-edited, but as discussion has usually centred on Guignard's introduction and texts, his edition has been retained as the basis in what follows. Its title will be abbreviated as *MP*.

abbots of the order in their annual general chapter. These three documents have been praised often and with justice, not only for their wisdom, strength and economy of words, but also for their authenticity and 'primitive' character. The *Exordium* and the *Carta Caritatis* in particular have been characterized respectively as a 'work of gold, small in bulk but great in weight and price'[1] and as 'a masterpiece, with a rigid economy of words and the utmost clarity of thought.'[2] Indeed, one recent and well-qualified scholar was ready to declare that it would be hard to find a religious order which possessed such a clear and simple account of its origins as the order of Cîteaux.[3] These judgments are still comprehensible, but whereas when they were written all scholars assumed as an unquestioned fact that these short pieces were pure and untouched metal, it has been shown within the past twenty years that the *Carta* and the accompanying *Instituta* are composite documents that have undergone serious and significant changes, and are the final issue of successive recensions in which much has been omitted of the original core, and much added to it, while the *Exordium*, though textually sincere, cannot be taken, at least without serious examination and rehabilitation, as the plain, unvarnished tale that it had seemed to be to historians of the past. The critical work that has effected this revolutionary change of attitude was

---

[1] A. Manrique, *Annales Cistercienses* (Lyon 1642), I, p. 10.

[2] D. Knowles, *The Monastic Order in England* (1940), p. 212.

[3] J. B. Mahn, *L'Ordre cistercien* (2nd ed., Paris 1951), p. 41: 'Peu d'ordres religieux possèdent une histoire de leurs origines aussi clair et simple que l'ordre cistercien.'

begun and developed for several years by the Slovene scholar, the late Monsignor Turk, and continued by a young Belgian candidate for the doctorate, M. Jean Lefèvre. In our discussion, it will be well to begin with the *Carta Caritatis* (referred to as *CC*), since this is the basic authority for our knowledge of the early Cistercian constitution.

(i) The *Carta Caritatis*

The *Carta Caritatis*, a brief document containing some 1,600 words, has long been recognized as one of the very few epoch-making and revolutionary pieces of monastic legislation. Within it are displayed all the constitutional principles necessary for the establishment and maintenance of a monastic order, and though it was composed for the needs of perhaps half a dozen monasteries, nearly all in close proximity to one another, it was found adequate for a vast family of seven hundred abbeys, scattered over the whole of Europe and the Catholic Levant. Bearing as it does its own authentication, so far as words go, in the account of its genesis, it was always, until a few years ago, accepted as a homogeneous composition, the work of the second abbot, Stephen Harding, *c.* 1118, nor was there anything in the abundant manuscript tradition to disturb this opinion. The text was apparently pure, and after Guignard had printed his edition from MS 601 in the municipal library at Dijon, there was general agreement that the last word had been said. The Dijon manuscript, written in its various parts between 1191 and 1236, was of Cîteaux provenance and proclaimed itself to be the exemplar for the whole order with the inscription *ut praesens liber sit exemplum invariabile ad conservandam uniformitatem, et corrigendam in aliis diversitatem.*[1] The text itself, as Guignard showed, had been composed between 1173 and 1191, for it contains in its calendar the feast of St Thomas of Canterbury, who was canonized in 1173, but the day is not classed among those when there were two public masses and no manual work; this rank was attained by the feast in 1191. It was assumed very naturally that in an order which had always prided itself upon uniformity and authenticity in its directories the official approval given was sufficient evidence that the text of the *CC*, thus approved, must be that of the document composed (according to the traditional opinion) by Stephen Harding in 1118 and solemnly approved by Calixtus II on 23 December 1119. It was thus accepted by every historian and critic in the world of monastic history, including Dom J. M. Canivez, who had been appointed editor of the order's official collection of the statutes of general chapter,[2] at the head of which the *CC* stood.

The first breath of suspicion as to the primitive authenticity of the vulgate text of the *CC* had come early in the present century, when a Cistercian named A. Trilhe discovered in two Paris manuscripts a version of the *CC* shorter than that printed by Guignard. This discovery was not published until,

[1] These words may be seen in the folio of which Guignard gives a facsimile.

[2] J. M. Canivez, *Statuta capitulorum generalium ordinis Cisterciensis, I* (Louvain 1933).

after many delays, it appeared as part of the long document known as the *Exordium Magnum,* in a volume edited by Tiburtius Hümpfner and published at Vác in 1932. The *Exordium Magnum,* a long piece of Cistercian hagiography, dated from the end of the twelfth century and contained an account of the foundation of Cîteaux, along with this shortened version of the *CC.* Hümpfner drew attention to Trilhe's discovery, and expressed a hope that some day a primitive text of the *CC* would be discovered. Unless or until that happened there could be no certainty that the shortened version (labelled by the editor *Summa CC*) was derived from an original primitive text. It might well be simply an erratic and erroneous tradition. Little or no notice was therefore taken of Hümpfner's obscure publication.

Nevertheless, within six years (in 1938) the missing text was, so it seemed, discovered by a Slovene scholar, Monsignor Joseph Turk, a professor at the university of Laibach (Ljubljana), in MS 31 of his university library, a codex of the twelfth century. He instituted a search, and a second version of the same type turned up at the Zentralbibliothek of Zürich, MS 75. Turk described his finds in an article in Slovenian in a very obscure publication,[1] but he was soon compelled to escape to the West and spent the rest of the war in a Cistercian abbey in Switzerland, where he was able to continue his researches. He published his first study of the *CC* in Latin in the first volume of the periodical *Analecta S. Ordinis Cisterciensis* in 1945, following it up with a later essay

---

[1] In the periodical *Kapistran Nyomda,* pp. 5–10, 27–8.

in the fourth volume (1948, printed 1949) of the same periodical, where in the sixth volume (1950), which appeared after Turk's death, the manuscript was printed in full.

In these articles he showed clearly that a version of the *CC*, more primitive than that printed by Guignard, had been in circulation. Quite apart from the precise date of the Laibach manuscript, it was certainly earlier than the manuscript of *MP*, and clearly no-one could have had any conceivable motive for producing a text of an official and sacrosanct document such as the *CC* which did not in fact represent the existing practice of the order. If, then, such a text existed, differing from the vulgate, it must of necessity reflect an earlier state of things, and therefore itself be an earlier version of the *CC*. This conclusion was supported by the evidence of three other documentary sources. The first was the so-called *Summa CC* already mentioned, which was now seen to be a primitive version, not an abbreviation of the *CC* of *MP*. The second was the first version of the constitutions of the order of Prémontré, which had long been recognized as deriving from the *CC* but as differing from the text of *MP*.[1] The third was a series of four papal privileges confirming the *CC*. These were the bulls of Eugenius III[2] (1152), Anastasius IV (1153), Adrian IV (1157) and Alexander III (1163). The *CC* had first been confirmed in 1119 by Calixtus II, and though it was not unusual at this

[1] The relevant passages were printed by Turk, *Analecta S. O. Cisterciensis*, IV, pp. 142–3.
[2] ibid., IV, p. 94.

time to obtain a fresh confirmation of every kind of privilege from each successive pope, as a kind of renewal of an insurance policy, in the case of the *CC* only one pope (Alexander III) confirmed exactly the same document as his predecessor. In other words, the *CC* was continually changing.

In view of all these arguments Turk decided that his two manuscripts gave the version first confirmed in 1119, which he therefore called *CC prior* or *CC¹* by way of contrast to the vulgate version of *MP*, which he now called *CC posterior* or *CC²*. What then, according to him, were the nature and extent of the changes made in the *CC* between 1119 and the stereotype of the Dijon MS 601? They were, he said, of three kinds, viz., in general form; in order of the parts; and in omissions and alterations.

Whereas *CC¹* consisted of a short historical Prologue followed by a series of chapters with headings, *CC²* made no distinction of Prologue and chapters, but ran straight on. This undoubtedly helped to create the impression, which we know to be illusory, that this later version was the unpremeditated outpouring of the mind of Stephen Harding. Actually, it was the result of a sophisticated rearrangement which, contrary to what usually happens, had proceeded from the apparently complex to the apparently simple. In this process of simplification the order of the paragraphs had been wholly rearranged. Here once more the change was apparently from a disconnected series to a tightly bound whole, in which one idea, one decree, led logically to the next. *CC¹* enunciated certain simple principles without co-ordinating or subordinating them; CC^2 arranged them all in a logical sequence. Turk, indeed, in a passage which was to afford an easy target for ridicule in the subsequent controversy, rather fancifully speaks of the Platonic character of CC^1 and the Aristotelian nature of CC^2, and notes that between the composition of the former and the latter had occurred the discovery of the *nova logica* of Aristotle.[1]

What is more important than any schematic rearrangement is the number of significant differences between the two versions of the document. They reflect the changing conditions of the order. The most notable is the gradual reduction of the powers of the abbot of Cîteaux in favour of the general chapter and of the four (originally three, La Ferté, Pontigny and Clairvaux, without Morimond) 'elder daughters.' In CC^1, when the order was small and compact, and all the monks and abbots still felt the close tie between themselves and the community of Cîteaux, the original annual chapter was conceived as the visit of the daughter abbots to the mother house for an unusually solemn chapter of faults, so that they might be examined and, if need arose, corrected by the abbot and the 'whole community' of the 'New Monastery.'[2] So homely was the gathering, that if an abbot was ill, or needed at home to bless a novice, he was to send his prior to act for him.

---

[1] ibid., IV, p. 15: 'Charta Caritatis primaeva platonice, Charta Caritatis posterior autem aristotelistice concepta est. Hoc factum omnino cum evolutione philosophiae in Occidente cohaeret' etc.

[2] *Novum monasterium*, as opposed to *Cistercium*, is normal in primitive Cistercian documents, and was taken by Lefèvre as a touchstone of date. This, however, is scarcely justifiable.

A similar intimate small-family relationship was seen in the arrangements for the election of an abbot of Cîteaux. All neighbouring abbots who can be summoned and arrive within fifteen days are to counsel and assist the brethren in their election. The procedure for deposing an unsatisfactory abbot is equally primitive. The abbot of Cîteaux is to warn the delinquent four times, after which he is to inform the bishop of the diocese and his canons. If they fail to act, he is to step in. As for Cîteaux itself, if the daughter abbots see that things have gone wrong, warning is to be given by the three elder daughters. If this is unavailing, the bishop and canons of Chalon are to be told; if they do not move, all the daughter abbots are to depose the erring abbot of Cîteaux. As for visitation, in CC^1 the task belonged to the abbot of Cîteaux, who could fulfil it either in person or by deputy; there were no directions for the visitation of Cîteaux itself.

Most of these arrangements were gradually modified. As regards an election at Cîteaux, as at other houses, the abbots assisting are those of the daughter houses. For deposition, the obligation lies upon the abbot of the founding house, not upon the abbot of Cîteaux. The three elder daughters (La Ferté, Pontigny and Clairvaux) become four by the addition of Morimond, and the primacy of La Ferté which appears in CC^1 is abolished. Finally, all references to the bishop and his canons disappear from the statutes concerning the deposition of an abbot. After the repeated warnings the founding abbot (or, in the case of Cîteaux, the four elder daughters) is to take action, but in this event, the matter is to be left over till the next general chapter.

In short, what may be called the paternal family arrangement of Stephen Harding is gradually replaced by the streamlined rules which can be applied throughout a great order of several hundred members.

Such was the exposition of Monsignor Turk. His chief and decisive discovery was that the Dijon collection of documents, and in particular the *CC* of *MP*, was not primitive. He thus threw all the *Monuments primitifs* into the critics' acid bath.

His pronouncements, as may be imagined, fluttered Cistercian dovecotes to some purpose, all the more so since, during the war and early post-war years, access to collections of manuscripts was restricted and the interchange of periodicals slow. Turk, for his part, regarded his discoveries as epoch-making, not to say earth-shaking, and put forward his conclusions as certain. But when normal conditions returned, Cistercian scholars began an intensive turn-out of the archives, and there were soon important new finds. At first, these were all in Turk's favour. Thus at Poblets and elsewhere in Spain three more manuscripts of the *CC* appeared, resembling very closely Turk's *CC¹*, and manuscripts of the *Instituta* or chapter decrees were found in abundance. These were all thrown into the pool without much discussion.

Then, in 1950, a young Louvain research student, M. Jean Lefèvre, at work on a doctoral thesis on Cistercian legislation, became interested in the problem of the *CC* and worked upon the various manuscripts more intensively and critically than Turk. From 1954 onwards for three years and more the results of his investigations and reflections began to flow out in a widening stream of articles. His production became so rapid that the capacity of one periodical after another was exhausted, and in consequence scholars had to be on the alert in order to pick up the various pronouncements as they appeared. Neither Turk nor Lefèvre could claim to be a master of lucidity, and it was unfortunate that both should have chosen to splash their theories down before mature reflection had made it possible to select the important and permanent threads of arguments and drop the rest. In consequence their arguments are very difficult to absorb; there are repetitions and cross-references, and with Lefèvre in particular the affair begins all over again with every new article, while the essential texts, edited and re-edited, are scattered about all over the learned landscape. What follows is an attempt to give the gist of Lefèvre's conclusions down to 1957, when he ceased, temporarily at least, to add to the literature of the main controversy. His conclusions traverse Turk's pronouncements at many points and also widen the field very considerably.[1]

Lefèvre's discoveries, as has been said, were derived from a more careful comb-out of manuscripts

[1] There is no complete account of the controversy. That of F. Masai, 'Les études cisterciennes de J-A. Lefèvre,' in *Speculum*, XI (1957), pp. 119–23, is the clearest, though it is selective. Those of A. d'Herblay, 'Le problème des origines cisterciennes,' in *R.H.E.*, L (1955), pp. 158–66, and P. Cousin, *Précis d'histoire monastique* (Paris 1956), pp. 269ff., are less satisfactory. For a list of Lefèvre's articles, see above, p. 198.

of early Cistercian documents, and he was greatly helped at one point by a discovery made by Dom Jean Leclercq.[1] We have already seen that one document, the so-called *Summa CC*, long thought to have been a late précis of the *CC* printed by Guignard (Turk's CC^2), proved to have preserved the outlines of an earlier version (Turk's CC^1). Turk had noted this, and printed an early text, but had gone no further. Lefèvre now became interested in another document, the so-called *Summa Exordii*, also printed by Turk. This had the appearance of being a précis of the *Exordium Cisterciensis Cenobii*—the narrative of the foundation of Cîteaux—printed by Guignard in *MP*, and scholars up to and including Turk had considered it to be (as all before Turk had considered the *Summa CC* to be) a late document watering down the official account. Lefèvre, however, alerted by the discovery that *Summa CC* had been shown to embody primitive materials, looked more closely at his various bunches of documents, and, to give the gist of a complicated story, found that they showed the existence of three groups of manuscripts each made up of four documents as follows. The numeration follows the order of antiquity of the oldest manuscript of each group:

GROUP I	GROUP II	GROUP III
Summa Exordii	*Exordium Cisterciensis Cenobii*	*Exordium Cisterciensis Cenobii*
Summa CC	*Carta Caritatis* (CC^1)	*Carta Caritatis* (CC^2)

---

[1] 'Un ancien recueil de coûtumes cisterciennes,' in *R.H.E.*, XLVII (1952), pp. 172–6. The MS is Trent 1711.

GROUP I	GROUP II	GROUP III
Capitula (a few decrees of chapter)	*Instituta* (more decrees)	*Consuetudines* (more decrees)
Officia Ecclesiastica	*Officia Ecclesiastica*	*Officia Ecclesiastica* etc.
Dossier of Calixtus II (1119)	Dossier of Eugenius III (1152)	Collection of *MP*

Of these groups the third equals Guignard's *Monuments*, the second Turk's Laibach manuscript and its congeners, and the first a hitherto unknown and still more primitive group. According to Turk, Group III represented the dossier presented for confirmation to Eugenius III in 1153, while the second represented that presented to Calixtus II in 1119. In other words, the two latter groups were of the official documents of the Cistercian order at different stages of its evolution, and it was therefore natural to suppose that the third group was a still more primitive official collection. Lefèvre, with a wealth of complicated, but on the whole convincing, arguments, showed that Group II was the collection for Eugenius III in 1152–3, while Group III was a still later one, possibly of 1163. As for Group I, he saw in it the primitive dossier presented to Calixtus II in 1119, and printed it as such. The *Summa CC*, however, is clearly not itself the *CC* of a primitive date. If we wish to reconstruct that document, we must take the text of *CC¹* and isolate all of it that is covered in outline by *Summa CC*. Lefèvre, however, was ready to go a step further than this. He noted that in *CC¹* the three first paragraphs differed from the rest. They are written in the first-person plural, and read as the personal directions of an abbot to his own foundations—in other words, the directions of Stephen Harding himself to two or more of his daughter abbeys. They lay down:

(1) That he will exact no material tribute of any kind, but that he retains the care of souls.

(2) That the Rule is to be observed exactly as it is in the New Monastery.

(3) That all customs, books and chants, etc., are to be exactly the same.

We have then, according to Lefèvre, at least four stages in the evolution of the *CC*, viz.:

(*a*) The short edict written by Stephen Harding alone, at the foundation (probably) of Pontigny in 1114, when for the first time a foundation was made outside the diocese of Chalon, in which Cîteaux lay. This is deduced from the reference in the foundation charter of Pontigny to a *carta caritatis et unanimitatis*.

(*b*) Additions made by Stephen Harding and the general chapter of 1118.

Whereas the earlier edicts were preceptive, the following obligations are contractual:

(*c*) A fuller edition by the chapter of 1152–3 (i.e. *CC¹*).

(*d*) The final stereotype of, say, 1180 or so, printed in *MP* (i.e. *CC²*).

Such were the main conclusions of Lefèvre regarding the *CC*. On some points they may well be subjected to revision, but he would seem to have shown conclusively:

(1) That the *CC* of *MP* is a document standing at the end of a long process of evolution.

(2) That it originated in a simple monarchic arrangement which aimed at preserving uniformity while avoiding giving any offence to the diocesan ordinary, but that all subsequent additions formed an agreed contractual constitution between Cîteaux and the growing order.

(3) That in consequence Stephen Harding was solely responsible for the primitive paragraphs i–iii and for those only.[1] He may have had a controlling hand in the rest of the dossier of 1119 (*CC¹*), but the final *Carta Caritatis* (*CC²*) is not in any literal sense his work, though he had supplied the acorn and most probably had reared the young oak.

Indeed, when we analyse with care the details of legislation in the various recensions of the *CC* we begin to perceive a very interesting and hitherto unsuspected evolution in the Cistercian organization.

First of all, Stephen Harding, as sole authority, when making his first foundation, undertakes not to make the least material exaction, but retains the right to oversee the discipline. Then, as his daughters multiply, and houses are formed in different dioceses, he decrees an absolute uniformity in all respects between them and Cîteaux and commands the abbots to attend every year at Cîteaux at a chapter where

---

[1] These sections run in Guignard's text from (p. 80) 'Quia unius . . .' to (p. 81) 'quo modo libet retinere.'

they may accuse each other or be reprimanded by him. Here we have an interesting half-way house between the daily monastic chapter for instruction and reprimand, and the full general chapter for legislation and judgment. In the next stage of the *CC* we have a large family with grand-daughters and great-grand-daughters. At this stage the system of visitation and general chapter at Cîteaux is perfected, and elections are allowed for. The vertical mother-daughter relationship is stressed, but at the same time it is forbidden to any mother save Cîteaux to hold a general chapter. The business of election and deposition next becomes a problem, and there are stages in its solution: at first, the abbot of Cîteaux manages it all; next, it is a family affair among all the houses near Cîteaux; finally, general chapter becomes the court of record and appeal.

There follows the question of Cîteaux herself, which was left unmentioned till the death of Stephen Harding. Here the duty of visitation, election and deposition is first entrusted to three of the four 'elder daughters' (La Ferté, Pontigny, Clairvaux), with the primacy of La Ferté asserted; next, it is the same three on an equality; then it is the first four (that is, Morimond now being included) as equals; then, finally, the four drop out and responsibility passes to the general chapter.

These developments, which at present can be only glimpsed in this manuscript or in that, will perhaps appear in all their fullness when all the Cistercian manuscripts of Europe have been sifted, but even now a story has been revealed which has remained

unsuspected for eight centuries, but which has all
the marks of authenticity, not to say of inevitability,
as a far more comprehensible account of the evolution of a great order than the previous conception of
a legislator of genius issuing a code to his subjects.

(ii) The *Exordium Cisterciensis Cenobii*

Having thus settled the hash of the *CC*, Lefèvre
then went on to deal with a document hitherto
regarded (even by Turk) as sacrosant: the *Exordium
Cisterciensis Cenobii*. But before going any further, it
may be well to avoid confusion by distinguishing
between the various documents with similar names
in the collections of Cistercian origins. There are
three *Exordia*:

I *Exordium Cisterciensis Cenobii*. This is the narrative piece, beginning: 'Super exordium cisterciensis
cenobii. Nos cistercienses etc.' It serves as an introduction to the *Carta Caritatis* (*CC²*) in the official
collection of *MP*. It is known for short as the *Exordium
Parvum* (*EP*).

II *Exordium Magnum* (*EM*). This is a long document of Cistercian hagiography, known also as the
Liber de viris illustribus ordinis cisterciensis, and dating
from the late twelfth century. It does not essentially
concern us here.

III *Exordium Cistercii* (*EC*). This, a piece beginning 'In episcopatu lingonensi,' has long been known,
owing to its insertion in the monastic chronicle of
Mortemer composed *c.* 1155. In the past it had been

considered as a late and tendentious plagiarism of the
EP, and was called by Turk the *Summa Exordii*. As
we have seen, this formed part of the first and earliest
group of documents isolated by Lefèvre.

The *Exordium Parvum*, as has been said, had
always been regarded as beyond the breath of suspicion. It professes to be written by the first founding
fathers of Cîteaux—'Nos cistercienses primi huius
ecclesiae fundatores successoribus nostris . . . noti-
ficamus'—and embodies a large number of original
documents issued by popes, legates and bishops. It
purports to have been written in or around 1119.
Lefèvre, engaged on his work among the Cistercian
manuscripts, had his suspicions aroused by two
circumstances. The first was that in Turk's Laibach
manuscript the *Exordium* in its very first paragraph
contained a clause that was omitted in the vulgate
text of Guignard. It reads: 'nam viri isti [sc. the
seceders from Molesme] videntes se . . . hanc regu-
lam [sc. S. Benedicti] . . . minime custodisse, *et ob
hoc periurii crimen scienter incurrisse* etc.' The second
point was also connected with manuscript indications. His researches, as has been said, had disclosed
a group of early manuscripts in which the *Exordium
Cistercii* (Turk's *Summa Exordii*) took the place occupied by the *Exordium Parvum* in the later group,
which ultimately became the group of *MP*. In other
words, the *EP* of Guignard was not an absolutely
primitive text, and the *EC* (*Summa Exordii*) was not
a late plagiarism of *EP* but an earlier version of that
document.

Lefèvre then put both documents under the microscope and came to the conclusion:

(1) That the *EC* (*Summa Exordii*) was the original account, composed at latest in 1118/19 for presentation to Calixtus II.

(2) That the *EP* was a propagandist document written *c*. 1152 and presented to Eugenius III.

(3) That the documents in *EP* were genuine, though arranged of set purpose out of order at least in one important respect. Hence, if carefully considered, they would be found to support the truthful narrative of *EC* as against the tendentious and propagandist *EP*.

The argument is long and complicated, and need not be summarized here. But it is natural to ask what reason there could have been for substituting another account for the *EC*, if this was indeed the primitive text. It was done, answers Lefèvre, to silence the Cluniacs who were saying that Cîteaux was conceived in the original sin of apostasy. The first founders had left Molesme, abbot and all, without canonical permission, and this was proved by the fact that Abbot Robert has been commanded to go back and had been followed by at least half the community. Lefèvre asks us to look at the first paragraph of *EP* in which the document is advertised as showing 'quam canonice, quanta auctoritate, quibusque temporibus' Cîteaux began, and stresses that by remaining at Molesme they were knowingly incurring the charge of perjury for breaking the Rule they had vowed to keep. In other words, *EP* is a tendentious composition which endeavours to give canonical regularity to an essentially irregular act by posing as a subcontemporary account supported by original documents. *EC* on the other hand is a straightforward chronological account with no bias in any direction.

It will be seen that this theory of Lefèvre is much less innocuous than that concerning the *Carta Caritatis*. In the case of the *Carta* the error, if error there has been, is the purely accidental error of mistaking a late document for a primitive one, and a slow process for a sudden flash of genius. In the case of the *Exordium*, on the other hand, if Lefèvre is right, there was a conscious and permanent act of deceit by which a solemn document, purporting to be the evidence of eyewitnesses, was forged for purposes of controversy and successfully inserted as part of the primeval heritage of the order's legislation. But Lefèvre has not made out a cast-iron case for his theory. He has not proved that *EP* was not composed before *c.* 1151, nor has he proved that *EC* was certainly in existence as early as 1119. He has not fully faced the difficulty that the whole Cistercian general chapter and community of Cîteaux, including St Bernard and many others of known probity and intelligence, should have been willing to accept and to insert in their official dossier a new and spurious version of their origins. The forged monastic charters that were not uncommon in the period are far from giving a valid parallel. Nor has Lefèvre proved to satisfaction the motive he alleges. He is not a monastic historian, and in more than one place fails to capture the mental climate of the time of which he is writing.

The decades of the bitterest feeling between the black monks and the white were over long before 1150, and there is no other evidence that at that time attacks were being made on the irregularity of the Cistercian origins. Nor, on the other hand, is it true to say that the Cistercian charges against the black monks were not expressed at the time of the first secession from Molesme. There is an oblique reference to their fear of being perjured breakers of their vows even in *EC*,[1] and there are explicit charges against Molesme in the account given in the papal legate's letter, which Lefèvre accepts as genuine, though he remains silent on the subject of this important clause.

On the other hand, there are difficulties about the *EP* in its traditional form. Even in the years when I myself, in common with all other historians of the period, accepted without question the authenticity of the document, I remember feeling that this emphatic assertion of contemporary witness was almost too good to be true. Looked at less complacently than before, there are serious difficulties in it as it stands. Who, in 1119, that is, twenty years after the exodus, who are these 'We Cistercians,' who want to bear witness how perfectly everything was done in those days? Stephen Harding and perhaps a few others were still alive, but would they speak like this? And to whom were they speaking? And if, as is probable, the document itself bears witness to Stephen's good qualities, who then are its authors? And why the

[1] cf. *Summa CC* [*EC*], ed. Lefèvre, in *C.O.C.R.* (Rome & Westmalle), XVI, pt ii (1954), p. 97: 'Inter se [sc. the seceders] tractant qualiter illum versiculum adimpleant. Reddam tibi vota mea quae distinxerunt labia mea.'

omission, in the vulgate text, of that significant reference to perjury incurred by a breach of the Rule to which vows had been taken? I confess that I cannot answer these questions, but I remain unconvinced by Lefèvre's arguments, and it may be worth noting that three scholars, J. B. Van Damme, Dom Winandy[1] and M. Charles Dereine,[2] all well known as experts on medieval religious history, have expressed dissatisfaction for different reasons.

There remains the third early Cistercian document, the decrees of general chapter. Here again the simple outlook of Guignard has been challenged conclusively by both Turk and Lefèvre, and it has been shown that few of the decrees were primitive, and that they were being continually augmented. The evidence here, however, is extraordinarily complicated and inconclusive as to details, though the general impression is clear. It is ironically unfortunate that Dom Canivez's great critical edition of the Cistercian statutes from the origin to the end of the Middle Ages should have appeared only a few years before the first volume was entirely antiquated by the new findings.

The winds of controversy have died down during the last three or four years. M. Lefèvre, it is understood, has not entered academic life but has adopted another profession, and his promised survey of the whole field has never appeared. Historians who would make themselves familiar with the arguments on this

[1] J. Winandy, 'Les origines de Cîteaux et les travaux de M. Lefèvre,' in *Rev.Bén.*, LXVII (1957), pp. 49–76; J. B. Van Damme, 'Autour des origines cisterciennes,' in *C.O.C.R.*, XX (1958), pp. 56–168, 379–90.

[2] 'La fondation de Cîteaux,' in *Cîteaux* (Westmalle), X (1959), pp. 125–39.

matter must therefore go through the very trying exercise of assembling and then mastering his scattered and ill-digested articles. Whatever we may think of some of his conclusions, he has left his mark on the *Monuments primitifs*, and the history of the Cistercian origins will never again be the simple story that has been repeated by all historians and writers for eight hundred years. Those who framed the *Carta Caritatis* in its vulgate form were successful in putting their version of things across to their world; the discovery of part, at least, of the true story is a notable achievement of the critical historian.

The criticism of early Cistercian documents has followed a different course from that of the Rule of St Benedict. Whereas the latter enlisted the talents of a number of distinguished and expert scholars, of whom the majority were Benedictine monks, the latter has for all practical purposes been conducted by two critics in succession, Monsignor Turk and M. Lefèvre, neither of whom was a Cistercian. Moreover, though each has undoubtedly left his mark on Cistercian historiography, neither Turk nor Lefèvre has shown himself a master of all the exercises of a scholar's craft. Both have been over-eager to publish their discoveries before they had been fully digested and screened, both in consequence have used an unconscionable quantity of space on matter that should have been severely sifted and ordered before the production of the finished article for publication, and both have shown themselves disorderly writers and impulsive judges. Turk passed early from the scene, and fared hardly at the hands of his successor, and it would seem likely that M. Lefèvre also, though still young, has said all that he has to say on the subject. Perhaps we shall not get much further until a scholar of the calibre of Dom Hallinger, let us say, or Dom Penco, takes up the matter again *ab ovo* and discusses it without *parti pris*. It is at least clear that before a final judgment can be expressed every effort must be made to assemble all available manuscripts of early Cistercian documents, with the aim of constituting reliable texts of the various stages of development and, if possible, of dating them either absolutely or in relation to one another. We know now that all the relevant documents were being changed, augmented and recopied throughout three or four decades, and it is of the first importance to be quite clear when, or in what order, the various versions appeared. The critic in his study or library can do little to help. The work is still at the stage when close work on the manuscripts is essential. To say this is not to decry the achievement of Turk and Lefèvre. They have shown once and for all that the development of the Cistercian constitution was not a sudden flash of a genius with foresight, but the response of a number of clear and statesmanlike minds to the unfolding of a difficult problem. Such a discovery is one more instance of the kind of revision that a critical historian is able to make in the history of institutions and ideas, and, as always, the facts thus revealed are more in harmony with the normal working of minds and institutions than was the original hypothesis of a piece of revolutionary legislation.

Postscript

THOSE who have read the two parts of this book may have reflected for a moment on the different ways in which critical scholarship may make its advances. In the great historical enterprises, co-operative association in various forms made available the raw material of history and in greater or less degree subjected it to comment and criticism. The positive end of printing documents or establishing canons and techniques determined the methods and the work, though criticism might play a large part in its execution. In the two controversies on monastic history the matter was opened by an individual's criticism of a received and venerable opinion. He was opposed or succeeded by others, and gradually a fabric of positive knowledge emerged which changed the outlook of historians on important moments of monastic development. Controversy and co-operation, the careful design and the individual intuition, are opposed in their character and appearance, but through each emerges a new realization of historical truth. Finally, in both these controversies we may salute the achievements of the spirit of enlightened critical skill. With no assistance save the documents under consideration, scholars of today have uncovered the real course of events which had been hidden for eight centuries under a delusive appearance of simplicity. 'What really happened' has, in these two cases, been revealed by critical analysis. Each is a notable instance of the results that can be attained by the internal criticism of a familiar text. And in each case, it may be added, the authorities and members of a great religious order have been content to allow their sons and confrères, and strangers without the gates, to debate the authenticity and significance of the most venerable documents, and even of those to which they have taken their religious vows. *Magna est veritas et praevalebit.*

Index

Index

Vanne, Congregation of St, 37
Venerandus of Altaripa, 143n, 165,
    186
*Veterum scriptorum amplissima col-
    lectio*, 51
Vígfússon, G., 118–122
Vitae Patrum, 6
Vivarium, 156, 161, 171

Waitz, G., 75, 76, 81, 82, 84, 132;
    as leader of the *Monumenta*, 83–5
Wattenbach, W., 77, 83, 84, 86,
    87

Weber, R., 153, 180, 185
Weiland, L., 81, 85
Williams ap Ithel, 126
Wilmart, A., 139
Winandy, J., 220
Winkelmann, E., 79
Wölflinn, E., 140

Yule, G. U., 156

Zeumer, K., 86
Zimmermann, O., 158, 171, 185
Zürich, 203

Printed in Great Britain by
Thomas Nelson (Printers) Ltd., London and Edinburgh

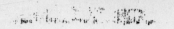